The Muvipix.com Guide to
Adobe
Premiere Elements 7
Steve Grisetti

The tools, and how to use them, to make movies
on your personal computer using the best-selling
video editing software program.

Dedication

This book is first and foremost dedicated to the wonderful people who have challenged, inspired and educated me with their questions, comments and support on the Adobe and Muvipix.com forums. Without you, I'd just be talking to myself.

And to my family, Jeanne and Sarah, who once again allowed me to focus on this little obsession for several months and offered their unconditional support and constant patience, even when they weren't quite sure what the heck I was doing.

And to the wonderful, hard-working moderators at Muvipix.com,whose ideas, solutions and shared knowledge have often helped me to appear a lot smarter than I really am.

And, finally, to my friends and Muvipix.com co-founders, Chuck Engels and Ron Hoskins. To Chuck, whose dear friendship, support and efforts in helping me get this book together are beyond measure. And to webmaster extraordinaire Ron, for always quietly and diligently working in the background, without whom there couldn't be a Muvipix.com.

About Muvipix.com

Muvipix.com was created to offer support and community to amateur and semi-professional videomakers. Registration is free, and that gets you access to the world's friendliest, most helpful forum and lots of ad-free space for displaying your work. On the products page, you'll find dozens of free tips, tutorials, motion backgrounds, DVD templates, sound effects, royalty-free music and stock video clips. Hundreds more are available for individual purchase or, for a small annual subscription fee that we use to keep the site running, you can have unlimited downloads from the ever-growing library of support materials and media. Please forgive us if we make frequent reference to this site throughout this book. We're really quite proud of the place!

http://www.muvipix.com

About the author

 Steve Grisetti holds a master's degree in Telecommunications from Ohio University and spent several years working in the motion picture and television industry in Los Angeles. A veteran of several video editing programs and systems, Steve has been with Premiere Elements since its introduction and, since 2004, has served as host for Adobe's Premiere Elements peer-to-peer support forum. He is also the co-author (with Chuck Engels) of *Premiere Elements in a Snap* and is co-founder of Muvipix.com, a help and support site for amateur and semi-professional video editors. He has taught classes in Photoshop and design, and he currently works as a graphic designer and layout artist for the in-house ad agency of a large, Milwaukee-based investment firm. He lives in suburban Milwaukee with his very patient wife and loving daughter, who wonder if he'll ever have more time to spend with them.

Table of Contents

Table of Contents

Table of Contents

An Introduction
To us and to this book

It's actually pretty amazing, when you think about it, how much you can do now with video on a home computer and just how easily you can do it. It wasn't that long ago that video editing, even for professionals, was a challenging, mechanical process involving dubbing and redubbing of tapes, lots of fast forwarding and rewinding and sometimes even physically cutting apart and gluing together strips of acetate.

These days the process is much simpler. You'll often hear modern video editing referred to as a non-linear process. That means we can grab your clips in any order you want from a photo album-like interface, rearrange them on a timeline, trim away what you don't need, add effects, titles, music – all without troubling yourself with the mechanics of rewinding or fast forwarding tapes or trying to locate a scene you want. And you don't even have to think about getting out a pair of scissors or a bottle of glue to do it.

Although I've experimented with several computer-based editing systems over the years, I was especially thrilled to find Premiere Elements. Here was not only an easy-to-use interface, but also a program that didn't skimp on features, offering production tools at an affordable price that were only otherwise seen on professional applications. Within a few months of my buying the program, I'd volunteered to host Adobe's peer-to-peer user help forum, and I've been with the program every version since version 1.0, doing my best to introduce everyone I could to the world of video editing and helping them to get up and running with this exciting, fun to use piece of software.

In early 2007, my writing partner, Chuck Engels, and I, along with webmaster extraordinaire Ron Hoskins, launched http://www.Muvipix.com, a help site and community of amateur and semi-professional videomakers. We hope you'll stop by, say hello. If you're at all serious about making great videos (or just having a lot of fun doing so), you won't find a better group of friends anywhere on the Web, and no finer supplement to the basic skills this book offers than the tutorials and tips in our products area.

This book, then, is the product of our years of experience with this great little program, with all of its advantages, powerful features, limitations, surprises and challenges.

Which brings me to a very important point about this book. At Muvipix.com, we believe in telling it like it is, when it comes to the programs we work with. So you'll have to excuse us a bit of editorializing here and there. If, for instance, we warn you that video directly from a DVD does not make the best source file for a Premiere Elements video editing project, we do so with good reason – and we'll recommend the best workarounds for making it work. After all, a video editing project can take days, weeks or even months of your life. We, at Muvipix, feel you deserve to know if there are liabilities in your workflow, even it it's not something you initially want to hear. Our feeling is that it's certainly better to be a little inconvenienced early on in your work by a few necessary conversions or a couple of tweaks than it is to put a good chunk of your life into a project that suddenly fails at a critical stage.

If you agree, keep reading.

Otherwise and regardless, we wish you a very happy and fulfilling moviemaking experience!

About This Book

When writing a book on any software application, you quickly find that there are a number of ways you can approach the subject. Many books are task-oriented, offering how-tos and step-by-step instructions for accomplishing certain tasks or creating certain effects. Others work as reference books, written less to be read than to be searched for answers.

In *The Muvipix Guide to Premiere Elements 7*, we chose to focus on the tools, features and functions of the software itself rather than the tasks that bring them into play. True, you'll find plenty of how-tos in here also, as well as tips and tricks for making the program do what you want it to do. But our main goal is to create a road map for the program itself, an attempt to reveal every major tool in this very powerful program and how to use it. A macro view rather than a micro view. Less a cookbook, then, than a culinary course.

Video editing is, after all, like any creative endeavor, about more than just performing simple tasks. It's about bringing your vision for your videos into fruition. And sometimes the best way to learn how to do this is to first know what tools are available and how each one works.

So maybe this book is really less a road map than it is a treasure map. We'll show you where all the buried treasure is hidden and how to uncarth it, but it's up to you how figure out how you spend your riches.

The book has been exhaustively cross-referenced so that, at nearly every tool, you'll find not only instructions describing how to use it but directions to related chapters or tools that supplement it.

And we hope you'll forgive the frequent references to products and further information available at Muvipix.com. This program runs very deep, and a book covering every possible function and every potential use would be as difficult to use as it would be write. So trust us that this is less a case of shameless self-promotion than it is a sincere effort to direct you to more advanced materials that we believe you'll find helpful in your goals.

Also, the forum at Muvipix.com is populated by some of the friendliest, most knowledgeable, most helpful people you'll find anywhere on the Web. And that kind of help, support and inspiration is available at no charge whatsoever. We hope to see you there!

Happy moviemaking!

Steve

Chapter 1

Getting to Know
The Premiere Elements 7 Workspace

The interface for Premiere Elements 7 has been designed by Adobe to be as simple and as intuitive as possible. It is also remarkably customizable, with a wealth of powerful tools in obvious and, once in a while, not so obvious places.

For the most part, Adobe's efforts to make Premiere Elements as user-friendly as it is powerful have resulted in an effective and efficient work area. However, some aspects of the default workspace can benefit from a bit of tweaking.

There are some panels, for instance, that take up way too much screen space, robbing valuable space from other panels. And a few important tools are harder to find than they should be. But a little customization of the workspace can go a long way toward making the best tools easier to get to and all of the tools easier to use.

For example, you'll notice that the program is laid out in rectangular panels, with many of the tools for each panel laid out as buttons or icons right on the panels. Now, before you do anything else with the program, *go to the Window drop-down menu at the top of the interface and select Show Docking Headers*! Do it. Now. Before you click another button on the program.

The Docking Headers are primarily there to allow you to undock the various panels – in other words, to separate the panels from the interface and position them some place else on your desktop. (To undock a panel from the program's interface, just drag it by its header.) This is particularly useful if you're using a very large monitor or even a two-monitor computer system. Spreading these panels out makes it much easier to get to all of the tools on each.

But there's another reason for revealing the Docking Headers.

The Monitor Panel

The multi-purpose Tasks panel

Docking Headers

The Sceneline

The Timeline

The Premiere Elements 7 workspace

Do you see the black >> buttons in the upper right of many of the panels? These buttons allow you to turn off or on a number of very important features and functions for that particular panel. In some cases, they also give you easy access to some great tools. But, unless you **Show Docking Headers,** you won't even *see* these buttons on many of the panels! (In fact, you won't even be able to see the names of the panels!)

So, whether you intend to undock any of the panels from the rest of the interface or not, activate the Show Docking Headers feature. You might well need access to what's otherwise hidden.

In any event, because of the size of the panels and the number of tools Adobe fits into some rather tight spaces, we wouldn't recommend this program be used on a computer with a monitor with less than 1280x960 resolution. There's simply no room for it all to fit otherwise, and you'll waste far too much time scrolling panels around, trying to get to all the tools. (The Monitor panel alone, for instance, demands at least 665 pixels across in order to display its entire playback and tool set – and even on a 1024x768 monitor, that doesn't leave much horizontal space for the all-important Tasks panel!)

In fact, in my opinion, the Monitor panel in Premiere Elements is way too large for the default workspace. There are also some less-essential panels large enough to block access to essential tools in other panels. Even on my very large monitor, for instance, I have trouble seeing all of the options under the Share tab at the default workspace setting. I also tend to use several video and audio tracks when I edit, so I make a point of widening the My Project panel (aka the Timeline/Sceneline) as much as I can, even at the expense of Monitor panel height.

So, once you've taken the essential step of turning on the Docking Headers, feel free to experiment and resize the panels by dragging on the borders between them. Or, if you've got a large computer monitor or, even better, a dual-monitor set up, undock the panels by dragging on their headers and moving them around your computer's desktop. (You can find out more about setting up and using a dual-monitor system in my *Steve's Tips* article "Setting Up a Dual-Monitor System", available on the products page at Muvipix.com.)

As you move your panels around, you'll note that there is one panel you can not undock from the program's interface. The Tasks panel (the multi-purpose panel which houses most of the program's functions) is locked to the interface. But, other than that, particularly if you've got lots of computer destktop space, you'll likely very much appreciate how much more accessible all of the program's tools are if you spread things out as much as possible.

And, if you ever do find the program misbehaving or if you just feel like you've lost control of your workspace, you can easily get back to the default look by simply going to the Window drop-down menu and selecting Restore Workspace.

Getting to Know the Various Panels
The major panels that are visible by default are the **Monitor** panel, the **My Project** panel (aka the **Timeline/Sceneline**) and the **Tasks** panel. We'll discuss each of these in greater detail as we explore the program's tools throughout this book, and we'll recommend a few other panels (available under the Window

The Monitor panel includes a toolbar for the playback of your video on the timeline and sceneline, access to the titler workspace and some valuable editing functions.

The Monitor Panel

drop-down menu and sometimes launched from buttons on other panels) that include valuable tools and you may want to manually open and keep open as you work.

The **Monitor** panel displays the video that you've assembled on your timeline or sceneline. The buttons along the bottom control your timeline's playback, while the tools in the lower right can be use for slicing clips, creating titles and grabbing a Freeze Frame from your video.

The Premiere Elements **Tasks** panel is your multi-function access point for the vast majority of Premiere Elements' workspaces and tools. Adobe has tried to make getting to each of these workspaces and tools as intuitive as possible by making the paths to them task-oriented. To gather your media, for instances, you click on the Organize tab and select Get Media. Your video editing tools are accessible under the Edit tab. You select and customize your DVD and BluRay disc menus under the Disc Menus tab and you output to various media or devices by way of the Share tab.

The Tasks Panel

Workspaces in the multi-purpose Tasks panel are accessed by following intuitive, task-oriented tabs and buttons

The **My Project** panel (which, most of the time, I'll refer to as the more apt if unofficial name, the **Timeline/Sceneline panel**) is where the actual assembly of your clips takes place. In Sceneline mode, you can quickly and easily assemble clips and add audio and transitions to create your movie. The focus here is on content more than how the elements in your video interact. Most veteran editors consider Sceneline a more elementary workspace for creating videos.

In Timeline mode, the emphasis is on time – not just what elements are included in your movie, then, but how and when they interact with each other. This mode is the much more traditional video editing workspace, giving you much greater access to Premiere Elements' true power.

In Timeline mode, you have a virtually unlimited number of audio and video tracks (officially up to 99 of each) as well as the ability to control effects, audio volume and the positions of clips (such as titles) that may appear on top of or share screen space with your main video clips. In short, if you have any interest at all in doing any really cool video editing, this is where you want to be. Trust us on this.

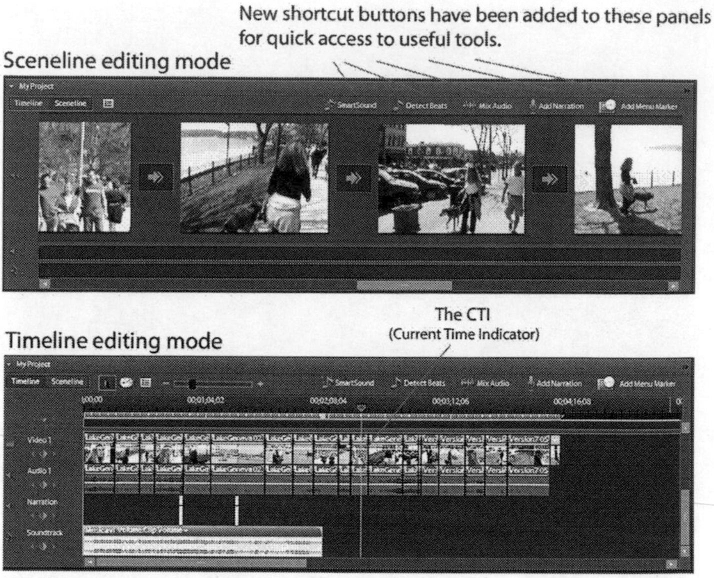

New shortcut buttons have been added to these panels for quick access to useful tools.

Sceneline editing mode

The CTI
(Current Time Indicator)

Timeline editing mode

The 'My Project Panel' (or, as we call it, the Timeline/Sceneline Panel)

What's a CTI?

Vital vocabulary alert! That thin, vertical, red line that moves along the Timeline as you play your video? It's called a **CTI**, which stands for Current Time Indicator. That's an all-important vocabulary term that you'll definitely want to know as we continue to work. (We've indicated it in the illustration above.)

Trust us on this. Especially since there's no other word that comes close to describing this thing, and we're going to use the term often throughout this book.

What's New in Version 7

Version 7 is less an overhaul of version 4 than it is a refinement of it. The interface itself is virtually unchanged.

(And, by the way, in case you're counting, there were no versions 5 or 6 of Premiere Elements. It's just that Premiere Elements has become continually more integrated and bundled with Photoshop Elements, which was developed a few years earlier and was leading it by a few versions. And so, rather than releasing version 7 of Photoshop Elements bundled with version 5 of Premiere Elements, Adobe has just decided that the "Elements Suite" should simply be deemed version 7.)

This new version boasts improved performance and greater stability all around (at least in our experience). It seems to handle a wider variety of file types more easily, and there are fewer of the hiccups that plagued some of the newer features (particularly the Text Animation for titles) introduced in version 4.

In addition, version 7 offers greater support for high-definition video. The program now supports AVCHD video as well as HDV and includes support for AVCHD's 5.1 channel sound.

The most obvious new feature in version 7's workspace is the additional of a fourth tab (Organize) to the Tasks panel. This tab serves as the access point to Get Media as well as to the new, more powerful Organizer and its tools.

The Get Media feature has been greatly expanded. Clicking the Get Media button under the Organize tab now opens an option screen which displays icons representing methods of capturing video from not only DV and HDV camcorders but also DVD camcorders, AVCHD cams, digital still cameras,

Get Media options in version 7

mobile phones and players and webcams, as well as the option to browse to media files on your computer. It's important to note, however, as we'll discuss in our chapter on capturing, that true, real-time capture can still only be made in Premiere Elements from miniDV and HDV camcorders. Clicking on the other icons (such as the DVD or AVCHD camcorder) launches the Media Downloader, the Adobe general purpose application for downloading photos from digital cameras or files from a scanner. Video from these devices is not captured in real time as it is with DV or HDV, but is merely downloaded as one or a number of complete media files. The exception to this is the Webcam option, which captures video into Premiere Elements from the live camera connection.

The Organizer in Premiere Elements 7 is now closer to the full-featured Organizer included with Photoshop Elements, complete with the ability to add Tags and then use them to sort and search your computer's media files.

The Organizer also includes a powerful SmartDetect feature that analyzes your clips and allows you to locate other media files that contain similar characteristics (e.g., find video clips which have similar faces, blur, motion and/or brightness). These gathered clips can then be directed to the InstantMovie workspace.

The new InstantMovie tool uses Themes (another feature introduced in version 4) to automatically create movies from any of its large library of instant movie templates, automatically adding music, effects, transitions and titles to your assembled clips based on the criteria you select or customize. (You can also go right to InstantMovie from the program's splash screen at the program's start-up, without having to launch the program fully into project mode.)

In addition to these new features, the Timeline has been slightly redesigned to include easier access to some of the program's previously "buried" features. A Mix Audio button launches the Audio Mixer, which allows you to raise and lower the volume for each of your audio clips, and a Clock icon launches a much more intuitive Time Stretch tool for slowing down or speeding up your movie's clips. The Detect Beats feature, which automatically places markers on the Timeline based on the

The new SmartSound feature creates custom musical tracks for your video based on criteria you select.

rhythm of the music you select, now places little musical notes on the Timeline rather than unnumbered markers – although they function pretty much the same way. And, in a concession to all of us who complained about how the all-important Properties panel was rendered all but invisible in version 4, this panel can now also be accessed from a button on the Timeline.

Finally, the program includes a new feature (even if it's a limited edition of it) that's long been a favorite of video editors. SmartSound creates custom music tracks based on criteria you select – giving you easy access to music that is the precise style and length that your project requires! The music sounds great, and a few clips are included with the program. Others, from their very professional sounding library, as well as a wide selection of sound effects, can be purchased as needed.

Photoshop.com
A highly visible new feature in version 7 is the program's ability to interface with Photoshop.com, Adobe's new photo and video sharing site. (A premium version of the site, Photoshop.com Plus, is also available, offering much more storage space.) Once

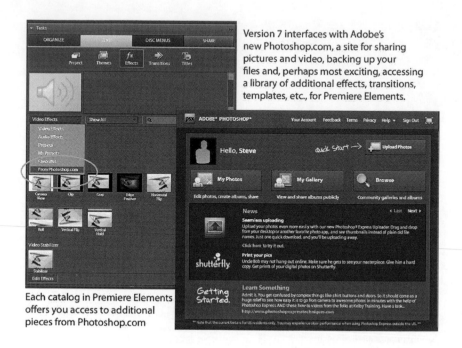

Version 7 interfaces with Adobe's new Photoshop.com, a site for sharing pictures and video, backing up your files and, perhaps most exciting, accessing a library of additional effects, transitions, templates, etc., for Premiere Elements.

Each catalog in Premiere Elements offers you access to additional pieces from Photoshop.com

you've signed on to this site, you'll find easy uploading to it through the Share tab, at the Online option. You also have the option of launching your computer's default browser directly to the site's workspace from the Premiere Elements' "splash screen", when you first start up the program.

The Flash-based site offers a variety of very attractive ways to display your photos or to play an "album" of your photos as a slideshow online as well as the ability to share and view your photos with other Photoshop.com members or through sites like Facebook, Flickr, Photobucket and Picasa.

You will also be able to back up your media files to the site – at least up to the capacity available. (Adobe gives you 5 gigabytes of space with the program. Additional space is available if you purchase a premium membership to the site.)

Additionally, Adobe plans to load bonus effects, transitions, title templates and other products onto this site for registered users. Once you create an account and set up an auto-logon at the program's splash screen, you'll be able to access these additional products seamlessly from many of Premiere Elements' panels and workspaces.

The Inspiration Browser

Finally, one more cool, new feature bears mentioning.

As you're working and navigating the various workspaces, you may notice little messages appearing in the lower right corner of the program's interface. Clicking on these messages will launch a link to the Inspiration Browser, your portal to a variety of free and useful tools for Premiere Elements.

(The first time you click on this link, you'll be prompted to install the free Inspiration Browser software.)

Adobe has partnered with a number of select, third-party providers who will offer free tutorials, tips, templates and other products through this portal and on this site.

Among those providers is none other than Muvipix.com, given the honor of helping support this great, little program. We hope you'll take advantage of this cool feature and enjoy some of the products offered through this link, supporting us as we continue to support Premiere Elements and its users.

Click on the lower right corner of the program to launch the link to the Inspiration Browser

Click on the pop-up link to launch the Inspiration Browser, a Photoshop.com page offering links to a wealth of tutorials and free products for Premiere Elements and Photoshop Elements

Chapter 2

Starting a
Premiere Elements 7 Project
Choosing the best settings

The "Splash Screen"

If you're a veteran of Premiere Elements, you'll immediately notice a difference as soon as you launch version 7.

The "splash screen" (the screen that displays when you first launch the program), which used to offer merely to start up a new project or re-open an old, now seems to be a workspace in itself! At launch, the program not only offers to open an old or new project, but it offers options for launching Photoshop.com or even to going directly to an InstantMovie.

Photoshop.com

Photoshop.com is Adobe's free online photo-sharing service. (A premium version, Photoshop.com Plus is also available for a fee.) You can create an account right here, at this splash screen. Once you've signed on and created an account, you'll be given 5 gigabytes of free display and file back-up space, which you can access here or under the Share tab inside the program, as one of the Online options. If you've got an always-on" Internet connection, you'll also automatically be logged onto the site whenever you start the program.

You can then access your posted photos by clicking the Web Gallery button. This launches your computer's web browser and directs it to your Gallery page, where you can create albums or add or remove photos or create very cool-looking, Flash-based online slideshows. You can also view the albums of other members or access the site's functionality with sites Facebook, Flickr, Photobucket and Picasa.There are tutorials also available from the splash screen that will show you more about this site and how to use it.

Launch InstantMovie   Open previous project   Start new project

Registration and autologon to Photoshop.com, a site for displaying
photos and from which Premiere Elements 7 accesses additional content.

The Premiere Elements 7 start-up or "splash" screen

But there's an even better reason to create an account and log
on here to Photoshop.com. As you use the program, you'll
see options on many of the panels to access additional effects,
transitions, title templates, etc., from this site. As we discuss
each panel, we'll show them to you. Adobe plans to continually
offer new Premiere Elements products from this site. Once you
create an auto-logon here at the splash screen, you'll be able
to access this additional content from Adobe seamlessly. It's a
great, free way to extend the tool set for this program!

InstantMovie

InstantMovie is the Premiere Elements tool for automatically
creating movies using customizable Themes, or movie templates,
in the program.

To create an InstantMovie from this screen, click the
InstantMovie button. You'll be prompted to name your movie
and select a location in which to save the project file. (You can
learn more about these options, including project settings, in
the discussion of **New Project**, below.)

Creating an InstantMovie

Clips are selected from the Organizer

Then a theme is selected from the InstantMovie Themes panel

More information on themes can be found in chapter 7, *The Themes Panel*.

Once you click Okay, the program finishes loading and the program's InstantMovie Organizer, will display the media files available on your computer. You can learn about using the Organizer to filter or order your media files in this display in **Chapter 4: The Organizer**.

Select the media clips you would like to include in your InstantMovie. You can select your clips either by holding the Shift key as you click on the first and last file of a group or by holding the Ctrl key and clicking to select your clips one at a time. Once you've gathered all of the clips you'd like to include, click the Next button in the lower right corner of the panel. (The program will prompt you if the clips you've selected aren't long enough for the Theme template to be applied to it.)

The Tasks panel will now display the library of Themes you can use to create your InstantMovie. The drop-down menu at the top of the panel (set to Show All by default) will allow you to filter the Themes displayed in this panel by category or to access additional themes available from Photoshop.com. You can see an animated preview of any Theme by clicking on the

Mix, match and customize theme options

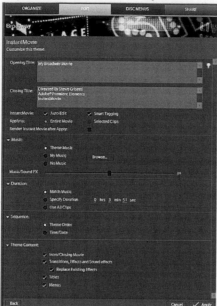

thumbnail displayed. Once you've selected a Theme, click the Next button in the lower right of the panel.

The Tasks panel will now display a list of the optional elements that make up your Theme's template. Type the titles as well as the names you'd like included in your credits in the boxes provided. You can then select or deselect which of the Theme's elements you'd like applied to your movie. You can even swap out music by selecting the My Music option and browsing to a music file on your computer. (You may need to scroll to see the entire list and click on the little white triangles to the left of the listed categories of options to see the entire options list.)

Once you've selected and customized the elements you'd like included, click the Apply button in the lower right corner of the panel. Premiere Elements will process all of the options and apply the elements you've selected to create your InstantMovie.

After the InstantMovie appears on your timeline or in your sceneline, the program will offer to render this clip for you. It's a good idea to accept this offer, as your InstantMovie will likely need to be rendered before it will play at full quality. The rendered video will provide you with a much cleaner representation of what your final movie output will look like.

(For more information on this process, see **Rendering** in **Chapter 11: The Sceneline/Timeline Panel.**)

New Project
Clicking the New Project button takes you to an option screen for creating your Premiere Elements project.

Starting a new project in Premiere Elements 7

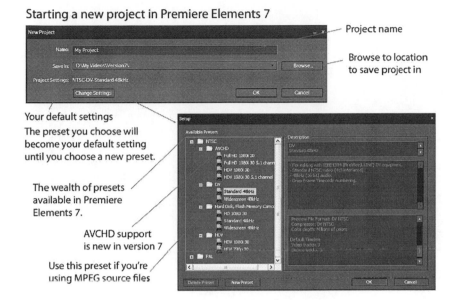

Project name

Browse to location
to save project in

Your default settings
The preset you choose will
become your default setting
until you choose a new preset.

The wealth of presets
available in Premiere
Elements 7.

AVCHD support
is new in version 7

Use this preset if you're
using MPEG source files

An important note about these project settings: They can not
be changed mid-project. You can not, in other words, decide
midway through your 4:3 project that you want to make it a
widescreen project. These, as well as the other settings listed
below, are only available when you initially begin your Premiere
Elements project.

Type the title for your new project in the box displayed at Name.

Click the Browse button to choose a location to save your new
project file.

We at Muvipix recommend always selecting Browse and,
wherever you choose to save your file, creating a new folder
especially for this file. This little bit of housekeeping keeps all of
your new project's files in one neat, little folder. And, when your
project is done and you want to clear it from your computer, you
can then remove not only the project file but all of the temp,
render and scratch disk files Premiere Elements has created for
that project simply by deleting that single folder! This makes
post-project clean-up a much easier and neater process.

Project Settings, at the bottom of the New Project settings, will display what you've selected as your default settings for a project. In most cases, you'll likely be working with the same settings for most of your projects. But, if not, clicking the Change Settings button will display a wealth of options.

In addition to the option for switching from PAL to NTSC or vice versa, this screen offers presets for a number of resolutions and video formats. Each of these folders, in turn, can be opened to reveal even more options, including the options for a widescreen 16:9 or standard 4:3 video frame and, in the case of the high-definition video settings, vertical screen resolution and audio channel format.

Setting your project up with the proper preset is essential to a smooth workflow and the highest quality output results, so consider carefully the nature of your source files as you choose your settings.

DV (standard or widescreen) – These presets are generally the standard workflow for the program. With these settings, the program interfaces with DV-AVI files, such as those captured from a miniDV camcorder.

Hard Disk, Flash Memory Camcorder (Standard, Widescreen and 1080i) – First introduced in version 4, these presets are designed to work with MPEG and VOB video source files, such as those from DVDs and hard drive camcorders. A project using these presets will automatically reverse the field dominance interlacing of these video files, allowing for a much smoother output from a Premiere Elements project. (For more on interlacing issues, see the discussion in **Using MPEGs and VOBs in a Premiere Elements Project** in **Chapter 3: Getting Media**.)

HDV (720p and 1080i) – These presets interface with MPEG2-based high-definition camcorders which, like miniDV, are tape based and stream captured over a FireWire connection.

AVCHD (Full HD 1080i 30, Full HD 1080i 30 5.1 channel, HDV 1080i 30 and HDV 1080i 30 5.1 channel) – These new presets allows for interfacing with video from MPEG4-based AVC high-definition camcorders.

New Preset will allow you to adjust some of the settings on these standard presets and save them as a custom setting – although Premiere Elements will only allow customization to a certain degree. The Elements version of Premiere, for instance, unlike the CS3 version, does not allow for the creation of a video project based on non-standard frames sizes or frame rates.

Once you've chosen the settings, name and location for your project, click Okay and the program will open to the project workspace.

Open Project

Clicking this icon will get you access to any work-in-progress or old Premiere Elements projects. Most recent project will appear in the drop-down menu. Additional Premiere Elements projects on your computer can be accessed by selecting the Browse option.

Opening a Project from Inside the Program

Naturally, you don't have to go all the way out to the splash screen to create a new project or re-open an old one. Both options are available from the File drop-down menu in the Premiere Elements workspace. Selecting New Project from this menu gives you access to the very same new project settings as are available from the splash screen.

Chapter 3

Getting Media
Into Your Premiere Elements Project

Before you can edit your video, you need to get it (along with your other source media) into your Premiere Elements project.

This is a relatively simple process but, unfortunately, one that can occasionally present some annoying challenges. Selecting the right input options and sometimes even converting your source files to a more optimal video format can definitely make this process go more smoothly. (For more information selecting the best settings for your workflow, see **Chapter 2: Starting a Premiere Elements 7 Project**.) In this chapter, we'll show you techniques for marrying the best video formats with the best project settings.

The sub-chapters below cover how to work with most of the current digital video formats in Premiere Elements as well as how to work with music and photos. For information on capturing from analog sources (VHS, 8mm, Hi-8), see **Capturing Through DV Bridges and Pass-Throughs**, below.

Why MiniDV is Still the Standard
MiniDV camcorders hit the market about a decade ago. Based on the professional DV compression system still used in broadcast video, miniDV camcorders record to a tape cassette not much bigger than a Zippo lighter, each cassette holding about an hour's worth of video at standard speed.

There have been many formats introduced since – hard disk camcorders, DVD camcorders, flash memory camcorders – but none matches miniDV in its ability to interface with computers and PC-based video editing system. This is as true for Macs as it is for Windows-based computers: *If you want to edit standard video on your computer, you want a miniDV camcorde*r. Trust us on this.

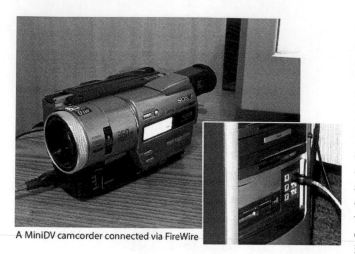

A MiniDV camcorder connected via FireWire

The chief advantage to a miniDV camcorder is that, when connected to a computer by a FireWire cable (also known as an IEEE-1394 or iLink), video data is not so much captured as it is streamed into your computer. The digital video data remains exactly the same as it flows from the camcorder to your computer (or back to the camcorder). The only change is that the capture software encapsulates the data into AVI files (known more accurately as DV-AVIs) or Quicktime DV files on a Mac.

Since the video data is not converted during capture, as it would be if digitized by a capture device, there is no change to the data itself, and hence no loss of the data's quality. This is an ideal data flow system: A computer in the camcorder conveying video data to your editing computer and vice versa.

Virtually all Windows professional style, computer-based editing systems are built around this DV-AVI workflow. When DV-AVIs are used in programs like Premiere Elements, they are not even re-rendered by the program (unless an effect has been added to them). This is not true of other video formats. This means that video from miniDV camcorders flows smoothly and efficiently through the editing process.

All miniDV camcorders have FireWire connectors, even if they also offer a USB connection. Our advice is to not bother with the USB connection, even if it means you have to buy your own FireWire cable. A few camcorders and some capture software will work with a USB connection, but with FireWire you'll know for sure you're properly connected.

Capture from a miniDV camcorder is also done in real time. That means that the capture software controls the camcorder remotely as you capture. You play the tape, you watch it on the Capture Monitor. You capture only what you want to use in your video project. What could be easier, right?

HDV (High Definition Video)

One of the most exciting video formats to become available to consumers in recent years is high-definition video or HDV. When configured to work with HDV, Premiere Elements handles the MPEGs from an HDV camcorder as smoothly and as efficiently as it does from a DV source. But remember: HDV is much more compressed and contains much more video data (approximately twice the horizontal and twice the vertical data) than standard DV, and that can put a lot more strain on your computer's resources.

The newest type of high-definition video is an even more highly compressed format called AVCHD, which stores the video data as MPEG4s. Version 7 is the first version of Premiere Elements designed to work with these files. However, that increased compression puts even more strain on your system, so it's very important to make sure you've got the resources to handle these files! Our **Appendix** offers our system recommendations for working with these more intensive formats and recommends tweaks for ensuring you're using every bit of power your computer can muster.

The process of capturing HDV in Premiere Elements is essentially the same as capturing standard DV:

The "Get Media" Feature

To bring media into your Premiere Elements 7 project, click the Organize tab in the Tasks panel and select Get Media. (There are other ways to get to the Get Media options, but this one is the most direct.)

At the Get Media screen, Premiere Elements offers eight options for bringing your media into your project, each represented by a brightly-colored icon in the Get Media panel.

The DV Camcorder, HDV Camcorder and Webcam or WDM Device options will launch the program's capture workspace.

Get Media options, under the Organize tab

The DV, HDV and Webcam or WDM Device options launch the Capture workspace.

The DVD (Camcorder or PC DVD Drive), AVCHD, Digital Still Camera and Mobile Phone options launch the Media Downloader.

The PC Files and Folders option allows you to browse to files on your computer.

You can also short-cut to Get Media options by right-clicking a blank area in your Project panel.

The program then interfaces with the video device, usually giving you remote control of the device and allowing you to preview the video in real time and select only the segments you want imported into your project.

The DVD/DVD Camcorder, Digital Still Camera, Mobile Phone and Players and even the AVCHD options launch the Media Downloader, Adobe's general input software for downloading photos from digital cameras or other devices. You will not have the option of previewing or capturing your video in real time with this software.

Capturing MiniDV, HDV Video or Video from Webcams or WDM Devices

The process of capturing video to Premiere Elements is virtually the same, whether you're capturing from a miniDV camcorder, an HDV (hi-definition) camcorder or even from a DV bridge

Three Ways to the Get Media Options

1. Click **Get Media** under the Organize tab

2. Right-click on a blank area in the Project media panel (under the Edit tab) and select the **Get Media** option

3. Select **Get Media From** from the File drop-down menu

(see **Capturing Through DV Bridges and Pass-Throughs**, below). Getting video into Premiere Elements from other sources, particularly over USB, is not quite so easy, and not without its challenges, as we'll discuss in **Using Other Video Formats** below.

To capture your video, connect your camcorder to your computer with a FireWire cable. When your camcorder is properly connected, powered on and set to play, Windows should register the connection (usually with a "bing-bong" sound effect) and a camcorder icon should appear on the right side of your Windows Task Bar. Windows should also launch an option screen offering you a handful of methods for capturing your video, among which should be Premiere Elements. If this is not the case, something is wrong, possibly at a mechanical level, and you'll need to troubleshoot your FireWire connection and camcorder set-up before you proceed.

Cancel out of this Windows option screen and, if you're not already running Premiere Elements, launch the program. In Premiere Elements, select the Organize tab and Get Video, then select the DV or HDV capture option. The Capture Monitor will open.

Although Adobe has overhauled the Capture panel in version 7 to make its options more easily accessible, the interface is intuitive enough that you can probably find your way around pretty easily, as you can see in the illustration on the following page.

If your camcorder (or DV bridge) is properly connected to your computer via FireWire, the panel will show Capture Device Online in the upper left corner of the panel and the Capturing Source drop-down should list the camcorder or DV bridge you are interfacing with. If not, you may want to try some of the capture troubleshooting steps at the end of this chapter.

With a proper camcorder connection, the playback buttons along the bottom of this panel will remotely control your camcorder. (If you're using a DV bridge or a pass-through, the source device or camcorder isn't connected directly to the computer, so these buttons will have no function.) Play, Fast Forward, Stop and Rewind you'll recognize immediately. Once you press Play, your camcorder's video should display in the panel and the Play button should become a Pause button.

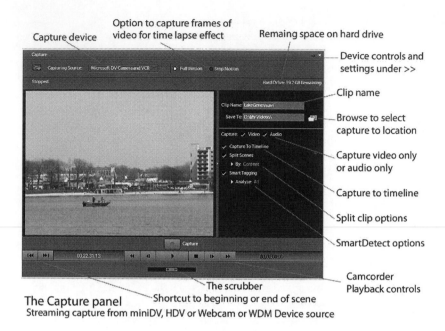

Capture device

Option to capture frames of
video for time lapse effect

Remaing space on hard drive

Device controls and
settings under >>

Clip name

Browse to select
capture to location

Capture video only
or audio only

Capture to timeline

Split clip options

SmartDetect options

Camcorder
Playback controls

The scrubber

Shortcut to beginning or end of scene

The Capture panel
Streaming capture from miniDV, HDV or Webcam or WDM Device source

The buttons to the right of Rewind and to the left of Fast Forward
are incremental advance and rewind buttons. They allow you to
advance or back up your camcorder's playback one frame at a
time. The slider under the playback buttons (called a Scrubber)
allows you to advance or rewind your video at a variety of speeds,
depending on how far you push it to the left or right.

At the lower left of the panel are two "shortcut" buttons.
Clicking on these buttons will automatically advance or
rewind your video to the last or next scene (the last point
at which your camcorder was stopped or paused). Premiere
Elements only reads these scenes when capturing from a
miniDV camcorder, by the way, so these buttons will not
function during HDV capture.

To capture your video, you simply use the playback controls to
locate the segment you want to capture and pause, then click
the Capture button. When you want to stop your capture, click
the Stop Capture button. It's just that simple.

To the right of the screen are the capture options. Type the
name you would like applied to your captured video in the Clip

Name space. (Premiere Elements will add numbers to the end of this name as it creates new clips during capture.) You also have the option of designating a location for your captured video from this session. By default, the clips will be saved to the same folder as your project file.

With the various checkboxes in the space below these options, you can designate that the program capture only audio or only video. If the Capture to Timeline option is selected, your video will be automatically added directly to your project's timeline or sceneline as it is captured.

The Split Scenes option allows you to set whether the captured video is broken into clips based on timecode (each time your camcorder was paused or stopped while shooting) or content (when the video content changes significantly). Since, when you're capturing through a DV bridge or pass-through, timecode is not being streamed into your computer from the video device, you can not split scenes based on timecode while using a DV bridge or pass-through.

SmartDetect is a new feature of Premiere Elements 7's embedded Organizer program. (You'll find more information on SmartDetect in **Chapter 4: The Organize**r.) Although the Organizer can analyze any media file on your computer, you can also choose to have the program analyze your video clips as you capture them, studying the files' content for things like Motion, Faces, Blur, Brightness & Contrast, etc. The Organizer can then use that metadata to select other clips on your computer with similar characteristics for an InstantMovie. (For more information on the **InstantMovie** feature, see **Chapter 2: Starting a Premiere Elements 7 Project**.)

Finally, at the top center of the Capture panel, you'll note that you have the option of capturing your video in Full Motion or Stop Motion. The Stop Motion option will allow you to set up the capture so that you grab frames from your video at regular intervals rather a continuous stream of video – the result being that the video will play very fast, as a "time lapse" sequence when placed on your timeline or sceneline. Set your Stop Motion, for instance, to capture only ever 30 frames, and your captured video will seem to play at 30 times normal speed. This is great for showing clouds rolling through the sky or the sun quickly rising and setting or a flower opening in mere seconds. Great visual effects, even if it does mean you go through a lot of tape to get a very short sequence!

Getting Standard DV from an HDV Camcorder

Just because you're shooting your video in high-definition does not necessarily mean you'll want to edit in high-definition. Unless you're planning to output your video as a BluRay disc or other high-definition media file, you can achieve excellent results on a standard DVD from your HDV cam by *downsampling* your HDV to standard DV within your camcorder before you capture it into Premiere Elements. The results, if a standard DVD is your end product, for instance, are actually much better than if you were to use HDV video for editing and then downsample it to standard video when you burn your DVD.

To capture downsampled video from your camcorder, connect your HDV camcorder to your computer via FireWire and set your camcorder to DV (called iLink Conversion or DV Lock on some brands) and capture into your Premiere Elements project (using standard DV project settings) as if from a miniDV camcorder. The video quality, although no longer in high-definition, will remain excellent, usually much better than you would get from a regular miniDV video.

Unless you're planning to create a high-definition output from your project, we highly recommend that you downsample your HDV camcorder's video in this manner and capture it as standard DV for the best results and the smoothest workflow.

Getting Video from DVDs and DVD Camcorders

Video from sources other than miniDV and HDV camcorders – including video from DVD camcorders and hard drive camcorders – is not captured into Premiere Elements. That is, it's not streamed in and captured in real time, as miniDV video is. Rather, video from non-tape sources, is downloaded into computer and your Premiere Elements project using Adobe's Media Downloader software.

To get video from a DVD or DVD camcorder, place the disc in your computer's DVD drive and select DVD (Camcorder or PC

Premiere Elements will only real-time capture video from tape sources, such as miniDV and HDV camcorders. AVCHD, as well as video from DVD, flash memory, hard drive and other non-tape-based camcorders, is downloaded, rather than captured, into the program by Adobe's Media Downloader.

DVD Drive) from the Get Media options. This will launch the Media Downloader.

From the Get Media From drop-down menu at the top of the Media Downloader, select your computer's DVD drive.

Click the Browse button to indicate where on your computer you'd like to save the DVD's files and click the Get Media button at the bottom of the panel.

If you're going to use video from a DVD in Premiere Elements, we recommend you use it in a project using the Hard Drive, Flash Memory Camcorder preset, as discussed in **New Project** in **Chapter 2: Starting a Project or Premiere Elements 7**.

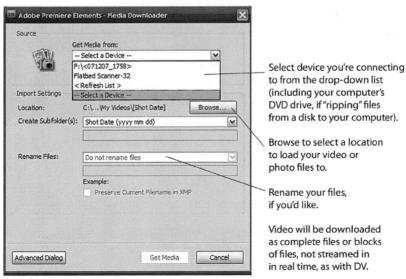

Select device you're connecting to from the drop-down list (including your computer's DVD drive, if "ripping" files from a disk to your computer).

Browse to select a location to load your video or photo files to.

Rename your files, if you'd like.

Video will be downloaded as complete files or blocks of files, not streamed in in real time, as with DV.

The Media Downloader
Adobe's general purpose software for downloading from cameras, scanners and other devices.

Getting Video from Hard drive and Flash Drive Camcorders

As with video from DVDs and DVD camcorders, the video from hard drive and flash drive camcorders is downloaded, rather than captured, into Premiere Elements.

To get video from these types of camcorders, connect your camcorder to your computer with a USB cable and select AVCHD Or Other Hard Disk/Memory Camcorder from the Get Media options. This will launch the Media Downloader.

From the Get Media From drop-down menu at the top of the Media Downloader, select your camcorder.

Click the Browse button to indicate where on your computer you'd like to save the captured files and click the Get Media button at the bottom of the panel.

If you're going to use video from a hard drive or flash drive camcorder in Premiere Elements, we recommend you use it in a project using the Hard Drive, Flash Memory Camcorder preset, as discussed in **New Project** in **Chapter 2: Starting a Project or Premiere Elements 7**.

Getting Video from AVCHD camcorders

To get video an AVCHD camcorder, connect your camcorder to your computer and select AVCHD Or Other Hard Disk/ Memory Camcorder from the Get Media options. This will launch the Media Downloader.

From the Get Media From drop-down menu at the top of the Media Downloader, select your camcorder.

Click the Browse button to indicate where on your computer you'd like to save the captured files and click the Get Media button at the bottom of the panel.

If you're going to use video from an AVCHD camcorder in Premiere Elements, we recommend you use it in a project using one of the AVCHD presets, as discussed in **New Project** in **Chapter 2: Starting a Project or Premiere Elements 7**.

Getting Video or Stills from Other Devices

To download video or stills from other devices into a Premiere Elements project, select either Mobile Phone and Players or Digital Still Camera from the Get Media Options.

From the Get Media From drop-down menu at the top of the Media Downloader, select your camcorder, camera or other device.

Click the Browse button to indicate where on your computer you'd like to save the downloaded files.

Getting Media from PC Files and Folders

To load video, audio or stills into your Premiere Elements project, click on the PC Files and Folders icon in the Get Media panel and browse to the file(s).

You can also quickly get media into your project by right-clicking in a blank space (below the media listings) in your Project media panel and select the Get Media option.

Other Ways to Get Your Video Into Your Computer

As we've said, Premiere Elements will not capture in real time from DVD or hard drive camcorders, including AVCHD camcorders. This can be a rather inconvenient way to get your video, particularly if you only need a two minute segment and the Media Downloader pulls down an entire 30 minute long file.

In the case of AVCHD high-definition video, Premiere Elements can work with the files as is, even if you use another program to capture the video. The video editing program that came with your camcorder will work just fine for capturing video from your camcorder. Additionally, some utilities that may have come included with your computer (such as Nero) can also do real time captures of AVCHD video.

Likewise, with MPEGs and VOB files from hard drive and DVD camcorders, you can use the software that comes with those camcorders to real-time capture your video. However, as we discuss in the next section, setting the program up to work with these files or, even better, converting those files to DV-AVIs can help ensure that you're using these files in Premiere Elements in the most effective way.

Using MPEGs and VOBs in a Premiere Elements Project

MPEGs and VOBs are essentially the same thing. VOBs are MPEG2s on a DVD.

They are both highly compressed video formats that provide excellent quality playback. Like DV-AVIs, they form video frames through interlacing – creating every frame of video in two passes, drawing every other horizontal line of pixels in each pass. This they do about 30 times every second (25 times every second on PAL video), too fast for your eyes to see.

The challenge is that MPEGs and VOBs usually create their interlaced frames with the *upper field* of lines first, while DV-AVIs create their interlaced frames with the **lower field** first.

That's not a significant issue *until* you bring an MPEG into a DV-AVI workflow, such as Premiere Elements. You may not see the difference when playing back your video in your project but, when you output your video or create a DVD from these types of files in Premiere Elements, the MPEG segments will often look very jumpy and jittery.

The old solution was to right-click on every MPEG clip on your timeline or sceneline and select Field Options, then Reverse Field Order. Very inconvenient and time consuming, if you've got a lot of MPEGs in your project.

But, in Premiere Elements 7, Adobe has provided project settings especially for working with MPEGs as source files – the Hard Disk, Flash Memory Camcorder project preset. (For more information on project settings, see the **New Project** discussion in **Chapter 2: Starting a Premiere Elements 7 Project**.) Video imported into a project using these settings will automatically have its field order reversed, and your MPEGs will render and output perfectly.

If you use MPEGs or VOBs almost exclusively as your video source files, this is the project preset you want to use.

Remember, however, if you mix DV-AVIs and MPEGs in the same project, you will have to change the field order for one of these video formats manually, as described above. Otherwise you may end up with a DV-AVI getting its field order reversed playing all jumpy and jittery on your DVD!

That said, although Premiere Elements 7 can work with MPEGs, VOBs and other video formats, the best – *the absolute bes*t – way to use these types of video files efficiently in Premiere Elements is to convert them to DV-AVIs. Trust us on this.

Converting Non-DV-AVI Files

For the cleanest results and smoothest operation in Premiere Elements, we recommend that, whenever possible, you use exclusively DV-AVIs as source files for your standard video projects.

If you're not shooting your video on a miniDV or an HDV camcorder, this may present a bit of a challenge. However, there are a number of very easy to use, very *free* programs available for converting almost any file to a DV-AVI, and we've listed a couple in our **Appendix**.

A favorite program for converting MPEGs and VOB files to DV-AVIs is the free utility **MPEG Streamclip**, from www.squared5.com. Instructions for using the program appear in the sidebar on the following page.

This process may seem a bit inconvenient at first. But the trade-offs in improved performance, trouble-free operation and higher quality outputs from Premiere Elements will very soon convince you that it's well worth the little extra effort.

Capturing Through DV Bridges and Pass-Throughs

There's a difference between a DV bridge and plain old capture device or capture card. Capture devices merely digitize your video input to any of number of video formats. DV bridges, on the other hand, are specifically designed to convert any video and audio input into DV-AVI files, the preferred video format for PC-based video editors. (Macs also prefer DV video, although they are saved as DV Quicktime files rather than AVIs. The video data content, however, is identical.)

Settings for Converting to DV-AVIs with MPEG Streamclip

To convert your MPEG/VOB in MPEG Streamclip, open the file in the program and then, from the File drop-down menu, select Convert to AVI.

For compression select the Apple DV/DVCPRO_NTSC (or DV-PAL, if appropriate) codec. Change the Sound setting from MPEG Layer 3 to Uncompressed and set the Field Order to Lower Field First.

If you have widescreen footage click on the Options button at the top right of the panel. Leave the Scan Mode as is but change the Aspect Ratio from 4:3 to 16:9.

Click on Make AVI and choose a folder and filename for your DV-AVI file to be saved to.

If you would like to save these settings for future use, click on the Presets button at bottom left of the panel, then click on the New button and name and save your settings.

DV bridges range from relatively inexpensive to high-end professional devices with time base correction and other video optimizers. The best value on the market in DV bridges and a Muvipix recommended "best buy" is the **ADS Pyro AV Link**, a favorite of many videographers. The Pyro AV link will take any AV input (a camcorder, a DVD player, a VCR or virtually any other video source, including live video) and port it into your computer as a high-quality DV-AVI file. This great device can be had for a street price of less than $150, a great value if you plan to edit a lot of video from non-DV sources.

Capturing video from a DV bridge is easy. Just plug your camcorder's, DVD player's or VCR's AV cables (RCA jacks) into the DV bridge's inputs and plug the bridge (connected by FireWire) into your computer. Windows will recognize the device just as it recognizes a miniDV camcorder connection.

The capture process itself is essentially the same as capture from a miniDV camcorder. The only difference is that, since there's no direct connection between your video source device and the computer, you won't be able to control the device with the

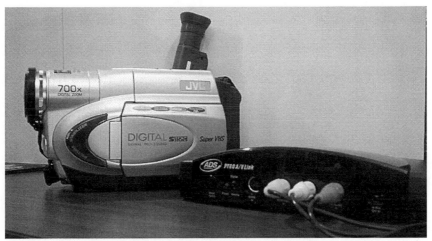

A camcorder connected through an ADS Pyro AV Link (a DV bridge)

Capture Monitor's playback controls. But, once you've got the device cued up to the segment you want to capture, you just click the Capture button and you're good to go!

By the way, the ADS Pyro AV Link can also be used with DVD camcorders and hard drive camcorders, so it's a great way to make any non-miniDV video 100% Premiere Elements compatible.

An alternative to a DV bridge is a set-up called a pass-through, which essentially uses a miniDV camcorder as a DV bridge.

To do pass-through capture, attach your non-DV camcorder to your miniDV camcorder, via its AV cables, and then link the miniDV to your computer via FireWire. With the miniDV camcorder in play mode (but without a tape inside) the non-DV camcorder's video then flows through the miniDV and into the computer, where it's captured as DV-AVIs.

The biggest challenge to using this method is that fewer and fewer new miniDV camcorders support pass-through connection. And it's very difficult to learn, from most spec sheets, which camcorders do. But, if your miniDV camcorder is pass-through capable, this is a simple and effective method of digitizing almost any analog video input.

Working With Photos

Premiere Elements can work with virtually any of the major photo or graphic formats, including JPEGs, GIFs, TIFs, vector art (EPSs and AI files), PSDs (native Photoshop and Photoshop Elements files) and PDFs. The exceptions are images using the CMYK color mode or RGB photo files using other than standard 8-bit color. But, if you are creating your graphics or using photos from a consumer graphics program (such as Photoshop Elements) or from a digital camera, scanner or other device, you don't need to worry about these exceptions. Virtually all photo and graphics files from these sources are compatible with the program.

Premiere Elements will also support transparency (alpha channels) so that file formats like GIF, PNG and PSD files with transparent areas will display, when used in a video project, with these areas transparent. This is particularly useful if you're using one of these graphics file types on an upper video track with a video layer behind it (see **L-cuts, J-cuts and Multiple Tracks** in **Chapter 11: The Timeline/Sceneline Panel**)) or as a graphic added to a title (see **Adding a Graphic** in **Chapter 10: Titles**).

Photos make great source files for a Premiere Elements project, but you'll find the highest quality results and the best performance from the program if the sizes of your photos are properly optimized before you bring them into your project. We urge you to make sure that any photo you use (especially if you use several in a slideshow) has been resized to *no larger than 1000x750 pixels* before you bring it into your Premiere Elements project to ensure the best quality and optimal program

Graphics and photo format

For photos, the most size-efficient file format is the JPEG. As an alternative, PSD files and TIFs use less compression and, though larger, also produce excellent results.

Because JPEGs are highly compressed, they do not make the best format for graphics which include clean, distinct edges, such as logos or graphics which include text. In these cases, PSDs, TIFs, AIs, EPSs and even PNGs produce the crispest lines.

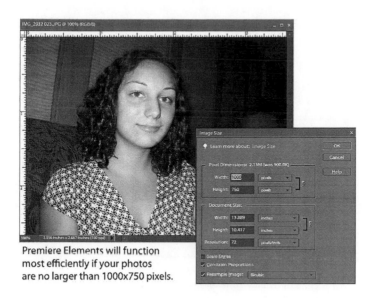

Premiere Elements will function most efficiently if your photos are no larger than 1000x750 pixels.

performance. (Photos taken directly from digital cameras can be 20 to 25 times that size!)

At first this may seem to go contrary to common wisdom. Traditionally, the higher the resolution of your photo, the better the quality of the output. But remember that Premiere Elements is a *video* editing program, and video is a relatively low resolution medium (essentially the equivalent of 640x480 pixels). And, to a point, reducing the resolution of a photo or graphic to be used in a video actually *improves* the quality of the video output. (1000x750 pixels seems to be that point)

The reason for this has to do with a process called downsampling, the system a video program uses to bring high-resolution photos down to video size. Premiere Elements does a fair job of this – but, as any pro knows, nothing that happens automatically will be as clean or as efficient as what you do manually. "Down-rezzing" is definitely one of these things.

There's also a more pressing reason for downsampling your photos yourself. The process of "down-rezzing", like the process of assimilating non-DV-AVI files into a video project, is a very intensive process. So intensive, in fact, that it's *the single biggest reason Premiere Elements fails*, particularly during the disc burning process.

Optimizing Photos for High-Resolution Video Projects

For high-definition video slideshows, the optimal size for a photo is 1600x1200 pixels – although note that photos at this size will put a bit more strain your system's resources.

It also takes a lot longer for the program to down-rez a 4000x3000 pixel photo than it does a 1000x750 pixel photo. Many, many times longer. And would you rather wait an hour or two for the program to transcode your DVD or 10 hours for a process that might end up with the program choking and dying anyway?

Trust us on this. Optimize your photo sizes to 1000x750 pixels before you import them in Premiere Elements. It will save you hours of anguish and misery in the end.

Photoshop Elements, by the way, has a very nice batch resizing feature that can resize a whole folder full of photos in just a few clicks. You'll find it under the program's File drop-menu, listed as Process Multiple Files.

Also, go *before* you do bring those photos in, go to Edit/Preferences/General in Premiere Elements and uncheck **Default Scale to Frame Size**. Left checked, Scale to Frame Size automatically sizes your photo to fill your video frame, giving a false representation of your photo in the video frame, and it can really get in the way when you're trying to add motion paths to your photos.

In the event this option was checked when you imported your photos into your project, you can also turn it off for your photos individually by right-clicking on each on the timeline and unchecking the Scale to Frame size option on the pop-up menu.

For more information on using photos and still graphics in your Premiere Elements project, see **Still Photos** in **Chapter 12: The Timeline/Sceneline Panel**.

Music Files

Although Premiere Elements works with a variety of audio file formats, you're probably best using exclusively MP3s and WAVs as your source files. They seem to provide the most trouble-free operation.

One word of warning, though, in connection with using music files in your video projects: Many music download sites (iTunes, for instance) employ electronic Digital Rights Management (DRM) in their downloaded files. This DRM system will throw up an error code if you try to load a copy-protected music file into your Premiere Elements project, blocking you from using the file.

There is software available on the Web for breaking this DRM. But probably the easiest way to get around this copy protection is to burn the music file to a CD and then use a program like Windows Media Player to rip the CD music file back to your computer as an MP3. The resultant MP3 should load right into Premiere Elements.

This process, of course, doesn't exempt you from respecting the rights of the artist who created the music however. So please don't abuse the privilege.

Troubleshooting Video Capture in Premiere Elements 7

Video capture from a miniDV or HDV camcorder seems like it should be easy. And, since you can't do anything in Premiere Elements until you have your video captured into your computer, when capture fails it can be very frustrating!

I wish I could tell you that there was a magic bullet for making all the problems go away, but sometimes there just is no simple fix.

The following, though, can help you troubleshoot your problems. And, if they don't work, the third-party solutions we recommend below will get you through the day (and may ultimately become your preferred workflow!).

1. Before you blame the software, make sure your operating system and its components are optimized and up to date. The computer regimen listed in our **Appendix**, and, in

particular, ensuring that your operating system, its firmware and drivers are up to date, is fundamental maintenance! Remember, you're using a very intensive program on an operating system that's constantly changing, updating and evolving. Like a race car driver who knows even a few pounds of pressure in one tire can mean the difference between a stable ride and one fraught with problems, you should always make sure your computer's operating system is in perfect working order. And always make sure you have the latest version of Quicktime and the newest RealTek drivers on your system! They may not seem obvious solutions to your problems, but more times than not, a simple update fixes the problem.

2. As mentioned above, if your operating system isn't even registering your camcorder as connected, you're dealing with a more fundamental problem than a Premiere Elements issue. Check your connections. Make sure your camcorder is set up right for capture (i.e., is in VTR/play mode). Possibly even check the camcorder on another computer to see whether it's the FireWire connection or your particular computer that's failing.

3. Make sure you're using a FireWire/IEEE-1394/iLink connection for capture. Some miniDV camcorders also offer a USB connection but, most of the time, they won't work with Premiere Elements. Trust us on this. You want a FireWire connection if at all possible.

4. If all connections are working and Windows recognizes your camcorder but Premiere Elements doesn't, note the auto-launch window that Windows opens when you plug your camcorder into your computer. What software does it offer to launch to capture your video? Some software (such as Nero) is less willing to share capture devices with any other software. And sometimes that means, unfortunately, capture directly into Premiere Elements may simply not be possible – at least not without way more work than it's worth. In that case, you may want to consider our third-party solutions below.

5. If all seems to be in order and Premiere Elements still isn't recognizing your camcorder, click on the >> button on the upper right corner of your Capture panel. (If this button doesn't show, go to Premiere Elements Window drop-down menu and select Show Docking Headers.) Select the Device Control option and, from the panel that opens, click on the Options button. This button will open another panel in which you can set the program to the exact brand and model of camcorder or DV bridge you're connected to. (There are Standard settings also, in the event your camcorder model isn't listed.) In all honesty, changing these settings rarely revives a dead camcorder connection. However, it can "refine" a connection in which the camcorder is recognized but capture doesn't seem to be going quite right.

Finally, if none of this works, you can use a third-party capture solution. Our **Appendix** lists some great resources for free or low-cost tools that can help. Our personal favorite capture software utility for miniDV capture is **WinDV**. This free and fully-loaded capture utility will often work even when nothing else seems to (assuming Windows sees the camcorder connection). Like Premiere Elements itself, WinDV captures miniDV video in small DV-AVI clips which are perfectly compatible with Premiere Elements and other editors.

Other options include the low-cost **Scenalyzer** and the absolutely free **Windows MovieMaker** (included with your Windows operating system). Both will capture your miniDV files in the DV-AVI format, which you can then import into your Premiere Elements project.

For high-definition video, **HDVSplit** is, like WinDV, free and yet very stable and nicely featured.

Because of the stability, reliability and sometimes extra features included with these free or low-cost utilities, many of our Premiere Elements users actually prefer to capture with these third-party applications and save Premiere Elements for what it does best – editing video.

Chapter 4

The Organizer
File management and InstantMovies

As we discussed in **Chapter 3: Getting Media**, the Organize tab is the access point to the Get Media functions of Premiere Elements. But this tab is also home to Premiere Elements' most developed new workspace – the Organizer.

Although still not as robust or as full-featured as the Photoshop Elements Organizer, the Premiere Elements Organizer in version 7 is much more sophisticated and powerful than it was in version 4. (My *Steve's Tips* article "The Organizer in Photoshop Elements and Premiere Elements and How to Use It", available from the products page at Muvipix.com, offers a detailed explanation of the Organizer's features and functions.)

Rather than being a separate, standalone program, the Organizer remains a sub-program within each of Premiere Elements and Photoshop Elements. But, as before, tags and other medata which you add to media files in one program's Organizer are also readable in the other. In fact, much of this metadata you create in the Organizer can even be read by the Adobe's Bridge program.

The purpose of the Organizer, as the name implies, is to give you an easy way to search, organize, categorize and manage the video, photo and audio files on your computer. Selecting the Organize tab on the Tasks panel displays thumbnails representing each of your system's media files. At this panel, using the various drop-downs, you can filter the files that are displayed by setting it to display only those files from a given Album (an album is created each time you start a project in Premiere Elements) or only those files which include a specific Tag. (More about Tags in a moment.)

Until you click the
Tagging button, the Tasks
panel displays a limited
version of the
Organizer workspace.

In this view, you can
filter according to tags,
ratings, date and
other metada using
the various drop-down
menus along the top
portion of the panel.

You can filter so that the Organizer displays only files to which
you've applied certain one-to-five star ratings to. (Check the
Details checkbox in the upper right of the panel to display the
Tags and Ratings which have been applied to your media files.
With Details displayed, you can also drag across the stars below
each clip to set a rating for your file.)

Below the Ratings filter, you'll see icons for filtering to display
only video files, only audio or only photos, or any combination
thereof. Clicking the fourth icon brings up an option screen
for filtering your media so that the Organizer displays only files
from a certain date range.

You can create categories and even
sub-categories of tags by clicking
on the + sign.

To apply a tag to any audio, video or
still file (or even several clips at once)
simply drag the tag from this panel
onto the clip(s).

To filter the Organizer to display only
clips tagged with certain keywords,
check the box to the left of the keyword.

Filtering buttons for display of only video,
audio, stills, tagged media or a date range

Albums are generated for each project,
but can be manually created.

Metadata added here
can also be read
by the Photoshop
Elements Organizer.

Tags can be dragged
onto a clip; new tags
and sub-categories
of tags can be created
by clicking the
+ button.

Clips can be
automatically analyzed
and tagged with
metadata based
on several criteria.

The Premiere Elements Organizer
Clicking the Tagging button under the Organize tab opens the full Organizer workspace

Tagging

Clicking the Tagging icon will launch the full-featured version
of the Premier Elements Organizer as a floating, undocked
panel. In this workspace, you can create and add metadata,
including Tags and Ratings for your clips, assign your clips to
Albums or use a variety of these and other criteria for filtering
which clips are displayed. You can also do some basic file
management here by right-clicking on the thumbnails of your
clips and selecting any of the various options.

InstantMovie

To create an InstantMovie, select any media files from the
Organizer – either by filtering or by holding down the Shift or
Ctrl keys as you select – and click the InstantMovie icon. You'll
be taken to the Themes panel so that you can select a theme and
set the options for your InstantMovie.

You'll find more information on using themes to create an
InstantMovie in **Chapter 1: Starting a Premiere Elements 7
Project**.

SmartDetect scans your clip and detects key elements, making it easy to locate similar clips for InstantMovies, etc.

SmartDetect
Analyzes and catalogs clips based on a number content criteria.

Smart Tags

Once you've finished creating your InstantMovie, the completed movie file will be placed on your timeline or sceneline, at the first available location. It's wise to accept Premiere Elements offer to then render the file before you play it back so you can see it at its full output quality. (More information on this process can be found at **Rendering** in **Chapter 11: The Timeline/Sceneline Panel**.)

SmartDetect

SmartDetect is a tool for analyzing any clip or clips you've selected from the Organizer, based on a variety of criteria (including Audio, Blur, Brightness & Contrast and/or Faces), in order to automatically create metadata. Once it has analyzed your clips(s), the tool will tag this metadata to your clip(s) and offer you the option of locating other clips with similar criteria. The tool will also offer you the option of directing these gathered clips to an InstantMovie.

Chapter 5
The Monitor Panel
Controls and features

The Monitor panels displays the playback of the clips you've assembled on the Timeline/Sceneline.

The majority if the controls available on this panel's toolbar, at the bottom of the panel, control playback. However, there are also a couple of valuable video editing tools here worth noting.

Playback Controls
You'll probably recognize the buttons for playing, rewinding and fast forwarding through your video. Additionally, between Play and Rewind, and between Play and Fast Forward, are buttons which look like this: ◀ and this: ▶ . These buttons will advance or rewind the playback of your video a single frame at a time.

One either end of the playback button set are the ◀ and ▶ buttons. These buttons will quickly jump you to the beginning or end of your current clip.

The numbers to the left of the playback buttons are timecode. This timecode represents the time position of the playback of your project. The numbers are displayed as 00;00;00;00, which represents hours; minutes; seconds; video frames. There are roughly 30 frames in each second of NTSC video and 25 frames in each second of PAL video. That's why that last set of numbers will only advance to 29 (or 24) before rolling over to zero again and advancing the seconds count.

To the right of the playback controls is the Scrubber, as illustrated at the top of the next page. This slider will advance or rewind your video at various speeds, depending on how far to the right or left you slide it.

The Monitor panel
Playback of Timeline and Sceneline, plus some editing tools

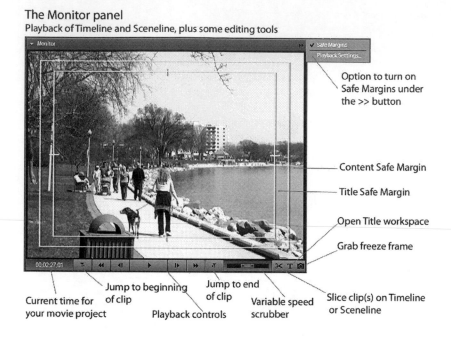

Option to turn on Safe Margins under the >> button

Content Safe Margin

Title Safe Margin

Open Title workspace

Grab freeze frame

Current time for your movie project

Jump to beginning of clip

Jump to end of clip

Playback controls

Variable speed scrubber

Slice clip(s) on Timeline or Sceneline

Split Clip

The scissors icon in the lower right of the panel is the Split Clip tool. Clicking this tool will slice through the clip(s) on your timeline or sceneline at the position of the CTI (Current Time Indicator), cutting it into two clips.

How this tool functions with several layers of video or audio clips depends on whether or not have you a clip on your timeline selected. If you have clicked on a clip on your Timeline (It will be highlighted if you have it selected), selecting the Split Clip tool on the Monitor panel will slice through *only that clip*. If you have no clips selected, the Split Clip tool will slice through the every clip on every layer at the CTI's position.

Add Text (Title)

Clicking the "T" icon in the lower right of the Monitor panel launches the Add Text tool (better known as the Title tool). Default text ("Add Text") will appear on the Monitor and the Tasks panel will display the Titles workspace. We discuss this workspace in much greater detail in **Chapter 10: Titles**.

Safe Margins

If you've selected Show Docking Headers from the Window drop-down menu, as we recommend in Chapter 1, you'll see the >> button in the upper right corner of Monitor panel. Click on it and you'll find the option to turn on your Safe Margins. Safe Margins will display as a pair of rectangular guides over your video display. (These guides will not be on your final output. They're just for your information.)

Safe Margins are great helps for ensuring that what you want to have on screen during your videos play will definitely be on screen in your final video output.

The challenge is that televisions can vary in how much of a video they actually show onscreen. All TVs cut a little off around the edges – and some cut off more than others. The purpose of these margins isn't so that you can resize your entire video so that it fits inside the inner margin, of course. But you should use them as guides to make sure that the *essential* video information falls within the "safe area".

The outer rectangular guide represents the Video Safe Margin. As you edit, you'll want to make sure all of the "must-see" video falls inside this rectangle. That means, for instance, if you're using a photo of a family reunion, make sure no important visual information falls outside this margin. Otherwise, well, you know that big group picture of everyone at the reunion waving to the camera that you've filled your video frame with? Well, some TVs may no show Cousin Bill, standing off to the side of the picture, outside the Safe Margin!

The inner rectangular is your Text Safe Margin. This is for your titles, subtitles and captions. *Never let your text be placed outside or extended beyond this margin.* Otherwise, some TVs may display your "Gone With the Wind" title as simply "one With the Win"!

Freeze Frame

The camera icon in the lower right of the Monitor panel is called the Freeze Frame tool. Although it might more accurately be called a "frame grab" tool, since it doesn't so much freeze a frame of your movie as it does create still photo from it.

Freeze Frame button on the Monitor panel launches Freeze Frame option screen.

Duration of still if added directly to timeline

Option to launch in Photoshop Elements editor

Option to export as a picture file

Freeze Frame options
Grabbing a still photo from your video

Option to insert still directly to movie's timeline or sceneline

Clicking on this icon brings up an option screen which displays the grabbed frame from your video (based on the position of the CTI on the timeline) as well as a number of options for saving it.

On this option screen, you can choose to simply insert the still in your movie. The inserted still will display in your video project at whatever duration you've indicated in Freeze Frame Duration.

Clicking the checkbox before clicking the Insert in Movie button inserts the photo into your movie and simultaneously launches the photo in Photoshop Elements. Once you've made any adjustments to the photo in Photoshop Elements and saved the file, the updates will automatically appear in the photo in Premiere Elements.

If you choose to save your frame as a photo file, we recommend that you change a couple of the default export settings in order to get the highest quality image from the file.

To do this, after you've clicked the Export button, click the Settings button that appears in the browers screen before you click Save. This will give you access to some very important hidden settings for your photo.

First, in Video settings, select the Square Pixels option from the Pixel Aspect Ratio drop-down. (Video uses non-square pixels, but photos with non-square pixels look stretched out of proportion.)

Then, in the Keyframe and Rendering settings, check the Deinterlace Video Footage checkbox.

Video is an interlaced medium. Every frame in video is created in two passes, with every other horizontal line of video data drawn with each pass. If you simply export your Freeze Frame as is from Premiere Elements, you will get a very jagged looking picture. This jagged look is a result of this interlacing.

Deinterlacing the picture essentially creates extra lines of pixels between these interlacing lines, ensuring that the photo you export from your video will be as clean and clear as a 640x480 pixel photo can possibly be.

Just another little nugget from your friends at Muvipix.com.

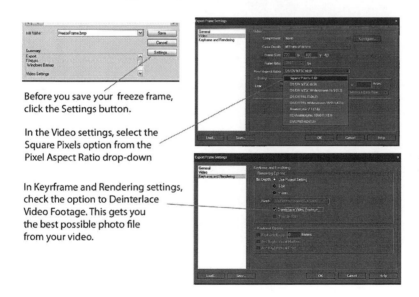

Before you save your freeze frame, click the Settings button.

In the Video settings, select the Square Pixels option from the Pixel Aspect Ratio drop-down

In Keyrframe and Rendering settings, check the option to Deinterlace Video Footage. This gets you the best possible photo file from your video.

Chapter 6

The Project Media Panel
Your Media Holding Area

If you select the Edit tab and click on the Project button, the panel will display a list of all of the sound, video and graphics files that have been captured or imported into your Premiere Elements 7 project.

The Project media panel is the catalog from which you'll draw all of the video, audio and still clips that you'll use to create your movie. To bring a clip from this panel into your movie, simply drag it from the panel to your movie's sceneline or timeline (as we discuss in **Chapter 11: The Timeline/Sceneline Panel**.) In fact, that's about 90% of what editing your video will consist of – simply dragging clips from here and placing them there.

But in addition to serving as a holding area for your video project's media, this panel includes a number of great tools for managing, ordering and preparing your clips for your movie's timeline or sceneline. The different viewing modes and folders make managing and keeping track of a large number of media files relatively simple. And the Clip Monitor is an invaluable tool for trimming your clips prior to adding them to your movie.

Displaying Your Media in Different Views
In the lower left corner of this panel, you'll see two blue icons. These are for switching the views of your media files from list view (the default) to icon view (which has the chief advantage of allowing you to drag them into any order you'd like – a valuable feature if you use the **Create Slideshow** feature, which we discuss below) and back again.

The Project panel

A catalog of the media files imported into your project

Filter to display
only video, audio
and/or stills

The New Item
button and
features

Clips are dragged
from here onto
the timeline or
sceneline

Media clips can be
more easily
managed by moving
them into folders

View as list or,
by clicking here,
as icons

Move up a folder level   Create folder

Folders

The two folder icons in the lower left corner of the panel are for creating and navigating folders in this panel. This is one of my favorite Premiere Elements features, extremely valuable when you're trying to sort through a large number of media files.

Click on the Folder icon to create a new folder, which you can then name. Once you have a folder created, you can drag your media files into it – sorting your clips so that all of your files for a particular segment of your project are in the same folder, for instance. You can even create sub-folders within your folders, so that it becomes very easy to manage and locate the files you need without having to scroll through the entire list of imported clips every time you need to locate a clip.

Even as you're editing, you can move your media around and in and out of folders to get them out of your way without affecting their positions or function on the timeline or sceneline.

New Item

In the upper right of the panel you will find a New Item icon which, when clicked on, offers a number of very valuable, short clips for your project.

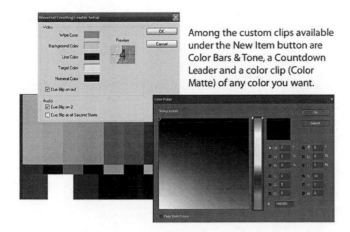

Among the custom clips available under the New Item button are Color Bars & Tone, a Countdown Leader and a color clip (Color Matte) of any color you want.

Title launches the Premiere Elements Title workspace. We explore this area more in **Chapter 10: Titles.**

Color Bars &Tone creates a clip of bars and tone, which broadcasters oftne require at the beginning of every video in order to calibrate their equipment to your movie's sound level and color profile.

Black Video and **Color Matte** create still clips of whatever color you designate, and which you can use behind titles or as blank spaces in your video.

Universal Countdown Leader creates a customizable countdown sequence (including an audio "blip" at two seconds) which can be placed at the beginning of your video — another feature broadcasters often require so that they can cue up to the beginning of your movie.

You'll also find a link here for launching **SmartSound**, the amazing third-party tool for creating custom, professional-sounding music clips for your project. For more information about SmartSound, see **Chapter 11: The Timeline/Sceneline Pane**l.

Right-Click Tools

There a also number of great tools available throughout Premiere Elements which can be (and sometimes can only be) accessed by right-clicking on clips or panels. I do a thorough

There is a wealth of great tools available via right-click menus.

Right-click on a clip for a number of tools only available here.

Right-click on an area of this panel beyond the media listings for quick access to the Get Media menus.

discussion of these tools in my *Steve's Tips* article "Powerful Tools in Premiere Elements' Right-Click Menus," available on the Muvipix.com product pages. Here are a couple of my favorite tools available by right-clicking on clips in the Project media panel.

Interpret Footage – Believe it or not, standard 4:3 video and widescreen 16:9 video use exactly the same number of pixels to create a video frame. The difference is that the pixels (the tiny squares of color that combine to create every frame of video) are shaped differently. Widescreen 16:9 pixels are much wider than standard 4:3 video pixels. Right-clicking on a clip and selecting Interpret Footage gives you access to options for conforming a widescreen clip to fit in a standard video or vice versa. This tool is invaluable if, for some reason, you find yourself with a clip that looks strangely squished or distorted.

Duplicate – This selection makes a duplicate of the clip you've right-clicked on. This is very helpful, for instance, if you've created a title slide with a style you'd like to re-use. You merely duplicate it and then revise the duplicate as needed.

Rename – You can rename a clip by selecting this right-click option or by simply by double-clicking slowly on the name of the file in the media panel listing so that the name becomes highlighted. Renaming a clip doesn't change the name of the file on your hard drive, by the way. Nor does it affect the clip's position or function on the timeline. But it can make it easier for you to identify the file later.

The "Get Media" Shortcut

If you want to import additional media from your computer into your Premiere Elements project, or even if you want to launch a video capture without going all the way out to the Organize workspace, you can open the Get Media menu right from the Project panel. Just right-click on a blank area of the panel, beyond the media listings, and select the Get Media option from the menu that displays, as in the illustration to the left.

The Clip Monitor

The Clip Monitor is a pop-up screen for previewing playback of a clip. It's also a work area in which you can trim a clip prior to adding it to your project by setting In and/or Out markers.

The Clip Monitor is launched either by right-clicking on a clip and selecting the Open in Clip Monitor option or by simply double-clicking on a clip. You can launch the Clip Monitor for a clip in the Project media panel or by double-clicking a clip on the timeline or sceneline.

When you set In or Out markers for your clip, only the segment of the clip between those markers will be visible during playback. In other words, if you have a 5 minute clip, you can set In and Out markers so that only a 30-second segment of the clip is actually displayed, rendering the clip essentially a 30 second clip when dragged to the timeline or sceneline.

In the Clip Monitor, the "live" segment of the clip is indicated with a heavier, purple area on the Clip Monitor's mini-timeline. You can adjust this live area's length by either dragging the end points in or out or by playing the clip using the playback controls at the bottom of the Clip Monitor and clicking on the Set In or Set Out icons to isolate the segment you want.

The Clip Monitor launches when you double-click on any clip on the timeline or sceneline or in the Project media panel.

Clips can be trimmed in the Clip Monitor either by dragging in the in and out points on the mini-timeline or by playing the clip and clicking the Set In and Set Out buttons.

Although the original clip remains its original length, only the "trimmed" segment (the purple segment in Premiere Elements) displays on the timeline.

The In and Out markers in the Clip Monitor can be used to isolate segments in audio clips as well as video. You can't set In and Out markers on titles and still images, however, because they are stationery elements.

Once the Clip Monitor has been launched, it will stay open as long as you keep your project open or until you manually close it.

Because this panel tends to pop up in the middle of the workspace whenever it launches, I usually launch it as soon as I open a project and position it off to the side and out of the way. That way, if I later need to open a clip in this panel for previewing or trimming, the Clip Monitor will play this clip where I've positioned it instead of in the middle of my work.

Once you've selected the stills from the Project media panel, you can launch Create Slideshow by clicking on the >> menu in the upper right corner of the panel.

Or you can right-click on your selected stills and select Create Slideshow from the right-click menu.

Set the order of the slides according to the order they appear in the media panel or according to the order you selected them.

If you've selected video clips for your "slideshow", you have the option of using the video only (no audio).

If you've created unnumbered markers with the Beat Detect feature, you can set the slides to change at these markers.

Apply a transition between the slides.

The Image and Transition Durations can be set by frames or by seconds.

Create Slideshow

One of my favorite automatic tools in Premiere Elements is the Create Slideshow feature. To create a slideshow automatically in Premiere Elements 7, you merely select a number of clips or stills from the Project media panel (by holding down the Ctrl or Shift key as you select) and then either right-click on them or click on the >> button in the upper right of the panel to access the Create Slideshow tool.

As you can see from the option screen that launches from this menu, you can set the order of the slides in your show in a couple of ways. You can simply have them appear in the same order as they appear in your Project media panel or you can have them appear in the order that you've selected them.

There are a couple of ways to put your clips in order in the Project media panel prior to launching the Create Slideshow tool.

If you set your Project panel to display your media in Icon View, by clicking the blue button in the lower left corner, you can drag to arrange your clips into whatever order you'd like prior to launching the Create Slideshow tool. Otherwise, in list view, you can order your clips by renaming them alpha-numerically so that they are listed in the order you'd like them to appear in your slideshow.

In the Create Slideshow option window, you can set your slides to change at a given interval of time. Or you can set them to change at Unnumbered Markers on the Timeline (More on that in our discussion of **Detect Beats** in **Chapter 11: The Timeline/Sceneline Panel**). You can also select the option to apply a Default Transition between them. (For more on setting the **Default Transition**, see **Chapter 9: Transitions**.)

You can use either video or still clips in your slideshow, although only stills can be set to change at a given duration or at the unnumbered markers created by the Detect Beats tool.

For information on how to optimize your stills for a slideshow, see **Working With Photos** in **Chapter 3: Getting Media**.

For more information on the tools and methods of creating slideshows using tools in both Premiere Elements and Photoshop Elements, and the advantages of each, see my *Steve's Tips* article "Creating Slideshows with Photoshop Elements and Premiere Elements," available on the products page at Muvipix.com.

Chapter 7

Themes
Movie themes for creating InstantMovies

Themes are a tool in Premiere Elements used for creating automatic or InstantMovies. (For more information on how to create an **InstantMovie**, see **Chapter 2: Starting a Premiere Elements 7 Projec**t.) They include a combination of titles, music and special effects that can be customized in a variety of ways and then applied to a set of clips you've gathered or selected.

In addition to their use in creating InstantMovies (which are created using clips gathered from the Organizer), Themes can also be applied to a sequence of clips already on your timeline or sceneline.

Applying a Theme to Clips on the Timeline or Sceneline
To apply a Theme to clips on your project's timeline or sceneline, select the clips on your timeline by dragging to lasso the clips you'd like to include in your InstandMovie. Once you've selected a group of clips, click the Edit tab in the Tasks panel and select Themes.

The panel will display a library of movie Themes. The drop-down menu at the top of the panel (set to Show All by default) will allow you to filter the Themes displayed in this panel by category or to access additional themes available from Photoshop.com. You can see an animated preview of any Theme by clicking on the thumbnail representing it.

Once you've selected a Theme for your InstantMovie, click the Next button in the lower right of the panel. The panel will then display the list of the optional elements that make up your Theme's template. Type the titles you'd like included in the boxes provided, then select or deselect the elements you'd like applied to

The Themes panel drop-down filters your Themes by category and gives you the option of downloading more themes from Photoshop. com

To select a sequence of clips on your timeline, just drag from beyond the end of your movie across the clips.

To preview a theme, click on it.

Click to select a Theme for you movie, then click the Next button in the lower right corner.

Once you've selected a Theme, you can customize it by including your own text and selecting which elements will be applied.

your movie. You can even swap out music by selecting the My Music option and browsing to a music file on your computer. (You may need to scroll to see the entire list of optional elements and click on the little white triangles to the left of the listed categories of options to see the entire options list.)

Once you've selected and customized the elements you'd like included, click the Apply button in the lower right corner of the panel. Premiere Elements will process all of the options and apply the elements you selected to the clips you selected.

After this automatically-generated movie appears on your timeline or in your sceneline, the program will offer to render it for you. It's a good idea to accept this offer, as your movie will likely need to be rendered before it will play at full quality. The rendered video will provide you with a much cleaner representation of what your final video output will look like.

(For more information on the rendering process, see **Rendering** in **Chapter 11: The Sceneline/Timeline Panel**.)

Chapter 8
Effects
Making magic from your raw footage

There is an amazing number of effects available in Premiere Elements 7 – too many, in fact, to display in one panel. The program includes over 90 video and 17 audio effects as well as a nearly 275 automatic, or Preset effects, that include applied effects as well as keyframed effects and motion paths, all of which are infinitely customizable. (For an explanation of keyframing and motion paths, see **Chapter 13: Keyframing**.)

In addition to these effects, the panel includes categories in which you can store your own custom created effects and motion paths (**My Presets**) and your most-often used effects (**Favorites**), for easy access. At the drop-down menu for each effect, you'll also find the option to access additional effects from **Photoshop.com**.

You can apply any number of effects to a clip. In fact, you can even double-up the same effect on the same clip (such as Volume on an audio clip) to increase its intensity. Sometimes the way effects interact with each other on a clip can create a new effect all its own. (For information on how to turn effects off and on for a clip, see **Turning Effects On and Off** in **Chapter 12: The Properties Panel**.)

Finding and Applying an Effect
Effects are displayed as thumbnails representing the effect's effect. These effects are stored within categories, and you can filter the listing of any type of effect to display a specific category by selecting that category from a drop-down menu at the top of the panel (which, by default, is set to Show All). You can also quickly call up an effect simply by typing its name in the search box to the right of the drop-down menus, as shown in the illustration on the following page.

The Effects panel in
Video Effects mode

The Effects drop-down
menu offers access to
the other Effects sets

The categories filter
drop-down gives you
quick access to any
category of effects

Quickly call up any
effect by typing its
name in the search box

Display effects by
thumbnail or list

Hover your mouse over
any thumbnail to
preview the effect

After effect is applied
click Edit Effects to
adjust it in the Properties panel

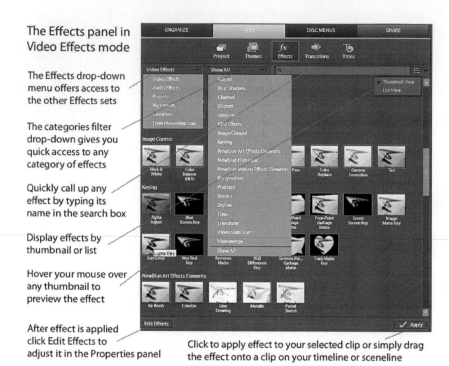

Click to apply effect to your selected clip or simply drag
the effect onto a clip on your timeline or sceneline

Applying an effect to a clip is as simple as selecting the clip on
your timeline or sceneline, selecting the effect by clicking on it
and then clicking the Apply button in the lower right corner of
the panel. (You can also simply drag the effect onto your clip.)

Some effects will cause an immediate change to your video. But
nearly all effects can be customized or have settings which can
or will need to tweaked once the effect is applied to a clip.

Settings for Effects and Properties

To adjust the effects settings, click to select the effected clip on
the timeline or sceneline and, from the lower left corner of the
Effects panel, click Edit Effects. This will open the Properties
panel for your clip. (You can also open this panel by clicking on
the clip on your timeline or sceneline and either right-clicking it
and selecting Show Properties or by clicking on Properties icon
(the list) at the top center of the Timeline.)

The Properties panel is a very useful and powerful workspace in Premiere Elements. With it you can not only customize your effect's settings (see **Adjusting Settings for Effects and Properties** in **Chapter 12: The Properties Panel**) but you can also create keyframed effects that change over the course of the clip or motion paths that move your entire clip around your video frame (as discussed in **Chapter 13: Keyframing**).

Video Effects

By default, when you select Effects under the Edit tab, the Video Effects catalog will be displayed. The video effects are arranged in categories, and you can use the drop-down menu to display only effects from one particular category.

Here are the various categories as well as brief descriptions of how the effects in that category work.

Adjust – The Adjust effects work primarily with color. These are the effects you'll use if you want to change or correct color in your clip. Additionally, **Lighting Effects** imposes a spotlight-like effect on your clip. **Posterize** reduces the number of colors in your clip, making it appear more cartoon-like. And the **Shadow/Highlight** effect is a great way to decrease contrast in a clip (e.g, the sky is too bright and the shade is too dark). Also available in Photoshop Elements, Shadow/Highlight is one of my personal favorite picture-saving effects!

Blur & Sharpen – These effects soften or sharpen your picture. The **Ghosting** effects leaves a very cool trail behind objects that are moving in your clip.

Channel – **Invert**, the single Channel effect, turns your video's picture to its negative.

Distort – The Distort effects warp, twist and/or bend your video image.

Generate – The **Lens Flare** effect in this category adds a bright, white flare to a spot on your video picture, as if a light is being shined back at the camcorder.

GPU Effects – These effects do some higher-end bending of your video picture, such as making it look as if it is a turning page. Note that these effects will only appear in your effects listing if your graphics card supports GPU effects.

Image Control – These effects offer tools for color and light adjustments. For more information on Image Control, including the default Image Control properties, see **Default Clip Properties** in **Chapter 12: The Properties Panel.**

Keying – Key effects remove or make transparent a portion of your video's picture. A powerful tool in this category is the **Chroma Key** effect, which we discuss in detail following this list. Other effects in this category are basically the Chroma Key preset to certain colors (**Green Screen Key, Blue Screen Key, Non Red Key**). Others, like the **Garbage Mattes**, create transparent areas in a clip that can be shaped with user-defined corner handles.

NewBlue Art Effects, NewBlue Film Look, NewBlue Motion Effects – These are great new image effects created by NewBlue, one of the world's top video effects companies. One of the most popular of these is the **Old Film** effect, a highly customizable effect which makes your video look like a damaged, worn, old movie.

Perspective – These effects can be used to make your video image look as if it is floating or rotated into space.

Pixelate – The **Facet** effect in this category reduces your video picture to a group of large color blocks.

Render – The **Lightning** effect is great fun, although it takes a lot of computer power to create and customize it! The **Ramp** effect fades your video out across the screen in a gradiated pattern.

Stylize – The effects in this category, as the category name implies, can be used to create a highly stylized video.

Time – Effects in this category change how your video displays motion by reducing or affecting the look of the frame rate. Note that this is not the place to go if you want to slow down or speed up a clip. That's the **Time Stretch**

effect, available by clicking on the clock icon on the Timeline. (See the discussion of **Time Stretch** in **Chapter 11: The Timeline/Sceneline Panel**.)

Transform – A real hodgepodge of effects, this category includes some stylized effects, some 3D transformations and, for some reason, **Clip** and **Crop**, two effects for trimming off the sides of your video picture. (For the record, Clip trims away the sides and replaces the area with color while Crop trims away the sides and replaces them with transparency – a significant difference, if you're using your cropped clip on an upper video track with another clip on a track below it). To learn more about using the Crop tool (or Clip tool, since you use the same method to adjust both) see **Types of Effects Settings** in **Chapter 12: The Properties Panel**.

Video Stabilizer – The **Stabilize** effect can be used to take some of the shake out of a handheld camera shot.

Videomerge – A new effect in version 7, this effect is essentially an automatic version of the Chroma Key effect. When applied to a clip, it removes what it interprets to be the background in a single step. It usually works very well, although like most "auto" effects, it benefits from having the effects settings tweaked in the Properties panel.

For information on changing settings for effects, see **Adjusting Settings for Effects and Properties** in **Chapter 12: The Properties Panel.** For information on keyframing effects to change over time, see **Chapter 13: Keyframing**.

Using Chroma Key

The Chroma Key effect actually appears in a couple of forms in the Key category of Effects. Variously known as Blue Screen Key, the Green Screen Key and the Non-Red Key, the function of the effects is the same – a color, or range of colors, on a clip is made to be transparent. The Green Screen and Blue Screen Keys are merely preset to the two most common "key" colors.

To create a Chroma Key effect you'll need two things: A video clip that has been shot with a subject standing in front of an even-colored, evenly-lit background (usually bright green or

The Chroma Key Effect

Shoot subject in front of evenly lit green or blue screen.

Place clip on Video 2 on the timeline and your new background on Video 1

Apply the Chroma Key effect to the clip on Video 2

Click Edit Effects to open the Properties panel

Click eyedropper to activate, then click on the Monitor image to select the background of your video as the color to be "keyed."

Fine tune the key (transparency) by adjusting the settings in the Properties panel.

blue, because these colors generally don't show up in human skin tones) and a clip with a background you'd like to swap in. You can only effectively do a Chroma Key effect in Timeline mode, because it requires two video tracks, as shown above.

Place the clip with the background you want remove (we'll call it your Key Clip) on Video 2 and the background clip on Video 1, directly below it. Apply the Chroma Key effect to your Key Clip and, with the clip selected, click Edit Effects or right-click on the clip and select Show Properties. In the Properties panel, click on the little white triangle to the left of the Chroma Key effect listing in the panel to open its settings.

Click to select the little eye dropper icon next to the color swatch. (The color swatch represents your key color, the color that will become transparent.) Your cursor will become a little eye dropper. Use it to click on the colored background in your Key Clip in the Monitor.

Once you've selected your key color, most of the Key Clip's background will become transparent, revealing your background clip, on Video 1. You'll likely need to do some fine tuning with the sliders in the Chroma Key properties to remove the Key Clip's background completely and smooth the edges between the keyed area and the subject in the foreground. But, if you've got a good, even-colored, well-lit background and an equally well-lit subject in the foreground, you should be able to make your key effect virtually seamless!

For more details on using the Chroma Key effect, see my *Steve's Tips* article "Working with Chroma Key," available on the products page at Muvipix.com.

An alternative to Chroma Key and a new feature in version 7 is **Videomerge**, essentially an automatic version of the Chroma Key effect. When applied to a clip (either by dragging or applying the effect from the Effects panel or by selecting the option from the clip's right-click menu), it automatically creates transparency in the area of your video image it presumes to be the background.

It usually works surprisingly well – depending, of course, on the composition of your video image. Although like most "auto" effects, it also often benefits from having its settings tweaked a bit in the Properties panel.

Presets

To access Premiere Elements' Preset Effects, click the Edit tab, then click the Effects icon and chose Presets from the Effects drop-down menu. The presets are represented as thumbnails in the panel and, if you hover your mouse over those that are animated, a preview of the effect will play.

Presets are, essentially, effects to which settings have already been applied. Some of these presets change the size or texture of your video clip or create a Picture-in-Picture effect. Others include keyframed effects so that the video image moves or changes scale or the setting for the effect changes over the course of the clip. (For more information on motion paths and keyframed effects, see the **Chapter 13: Keyframing**.) In fact, once you apply a preset to a clip, you can open the clip's Properties panel and adjust the settings or keyframe positions

The Effects panel in
Presets mode

The Presets drop-down
menu offers access to
the other Effects sets

The categories filter
drop-down gives you
quick access to any
category of presets

Quickly call up any
preset by typing its
name in the search box

Display presets by
thumbnail or list

Hover your mouse over
any thumbnail to
preview the preset

After preset is applied
click Edit Effects to
adjust it in the Properties panel

Click to apply effect to your selected clip or simply drag
the effect onto a clip on your timeline or sceneline

to tweak it. (For information on making these adjustments, see **Adjusting Settings for Effects and Properties** in **Chapter 12: The Properties Panel.**)

To apply a preset effect to a clip, simply click to select the clip on your timeline or sceneline, then either drag the preset from the Preset panel or click the Apply button in the lower right corner of the panel.

Preset Effects fall into a number of categories.

> **Bevel Edges** – These presets create the illusion of a raised edge along the sides of your video clip.
>
> **Blurs** – Blur presets go from blurry to clear or clear to blurry, and can be used to introduce or exit your clip. When using multi-track editing (**See L-Cuts, J-Cuts and Multiple Tracks** in the **Chapter 11: The Timeline/**

Sceneline Panel), you can use these keyframed blurs as transitions. To learn more on using presets as transitions, see my *Steve's Tips* article "Creating Transitions Using Presets" available on the products page at Muvipix.com

Color Effects – These presets can be used to tint your clip or increase the color saturation.

Drop Shadows – These presets reduce your clip's scale and create a shadow effect so that your clip appears to be floating – an effect that's most effective when applied to a clip on Video track 2, casting a shadow over a clip on Video track 1. Some of these presets use motion paths to move this shadow around over the course of your clip.

Horizontal Image Pans, Horizontal Image Zooms, Vertical Image Pans, Vertical Image Zooms – These presets are pre-created motion paths for panning and zooming around your photos, their names describing which size photo they are preset to pan or zoom across. They'll do the job in a pinch, but you'll have much more control over the process if you use keyframing to create your own motion paths, as explained in **Chapter 13: Keyframing**.

Mosaics – These presets will introduce or exit your clip from or through a mosaic pattern.

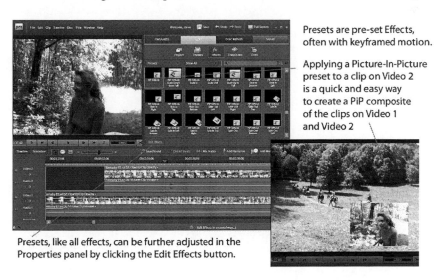

Presets are pre-set Effects, often with keyframed motion.

Applying a Picture-In-Picture preset to a clip on Video 2 is a quick and easy way to create a PiP composite of the clips on Video 1 and Video 2

Presets, like all effects, can be further adjusted in the Properties panel by clicking the Edit Effects button.

Picture-in-Picture (PiP) – The PiP presets, when applied to a clip on Video 2 with another clip on Video 1 under it, automatically reduce the scale of the clip on Video 2 and reposition it in the video frame, so that both it and the clip under it are both on screen at the same time. Some presets will even add motion, changing the scale or position of PiP over the course of the clip, sometimes using an elaborate animation, such as spinning.

Solarizes – These presets introduce or exit your clip with or through a bright solarize effect.

Twirls – These presets introduce or exit your clip with or through a twirl effect.

My Presets
You can easily create your own presets, saving your personal settings for an effect or motion path for future use. For information on saving a preset, see **Saving a Custom Preset** in the **Chapter 12: The Properties Panel**.

Applying a custom preset to a clip is just like applying a default preset. Click to select the clip on your timeline or sceneline and then either drag the preset from the My Preset panel or click the Apply button in the lower right corner of the panel.

Audio Effects
To open the Audio Effects catalog, click the Effects button under the Edit tab and then select Audio Effects from the panel's drop-down menu.

Premiere Elements 7 offers 17 audio effects which can be used to enhance your project.

A number of these effects (**Bass**, **Treble** and **Volume**) can easily be identified by their names. Others (**Denoiser, Highpass, Lowpass** and **Notch**) are filters for removing certain frequencies of sound. **Dynamics** and **Invert** are processors for "sweetening" your movie's sound.

Four effects adjust the right and left channels of your stereo audio. **Balance** raises or lowers the volume of each channel relative to the other while **Swap** switches the left and right

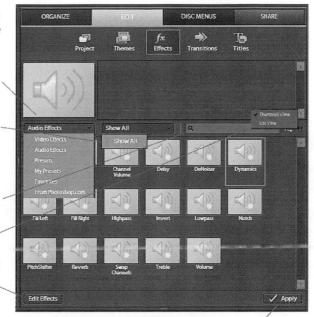

The Effects panel in
Audio Effects mode

The Effects drop-down
menu offers access to
the other Effects sets

Because there are only
17 audio effects, there
are no categories
of audio effects

Quickly call up any
effect by typing its
name in the search box

Display effects by
thumbnail or list

After an effect is applied
click Edit Effects to
adjust it in the
Properties panel

Click to apply effect to your selected clip or simply drag
the effect onto a clip on your timeline or sceneline

channel's audio. **Fill Left** and **Fill Right** are very helpful effects
for those times when you have audio on only one of your stereo
channels. Applying Fill Left or Fill Right takes the audio from
one channel and uses it for both.

Delay and **Reverb** create echo effects. The Reverb effect has a
number of great presets among its properties for making your
audio sound as though it's echoing through a small room, a
large church, etc.

The **Dynamics** and **DeNoiser** effects likewise offer presets
for affecting the sound of your audio clip (as seen in the
illustration on the next page). The DeNoiser is primarily
designed to clean up tape noise that may have crept into
your audio, while Dynamics lets you "sweeten" the sound
by removing some background noise, reducing distortion or
otherwise balancing the dynamic range. Well tuned dynamics
can give your video a richer, more professional, more big-
screen movie-like sound.

Some audio effects, like Dynamics, Reverb and Pitch Shifter, can be set using manual controls or by using presets from the drop-down list at the right end of the effect's listing in the Properties panel

And just for fun, there's the **PitchShifter**, which changes the pitch of an audio track, usually in very unnatural and often comic ways. The presets for this clip pretty much say it all: Female Becomes Secret Agent, Cartoon Mouse, Boo!, Sore Throat, Breathless, Slightly Detuned, etc.

As with video effects, audio effects can be applied constantly, for the entire duration of a clip or, using keyframing, you can vary the intensity or settings for your effects or properties over the course of the clip – making the audio louder in some portions of the clip and quieter in others, for instance.

For more information on changing settings for effects, see **Adjusting Settings for Effects and Properties** in **Chapter 12: The Properties Panel.** For information on keyframing effects, see **Chapter 13: Keyframing**.

As with video, there are also a few basic audio adjustments that can be made using the default properties which appear in the Properties panel – namely **Balance** and **Volume**. (See **Default Clip Properties** in the **Chapter 12: The Properties Panel**.) Additionally, audio levels can be controlled, and even raised and lowered at specific spots, right on your project's timeline. We explain how in **Adjusting Audio Levels on the Timeline** in **Chapter 11: The Timeline/Sceneline Panel**.

Chapter 9

Transitions
Exciting ways for getting
from one clip to the next

Transitions in Premiere Elements 7 are easy to use. However, like most of Premiere Elements' tools, there's also a surprising amount you can do to customize them, if you know where to look.

To open the Transitions panel, select the Edit tab and click on the Transitions button. You can access each of the Transitions catalogs from the drop-down menu. At this drop-down menu, you'll also find the option to load additional transitions from Photoshop.com.

Like many of Premiere Elements' tools, Transitions are arranged in categories. By default, the filter drop-down menu is set to Show All, displaying all 100 or so of the program's Video Transitions, for instance. By selecting a category from the drop-down menu, you can filter the list to display only the Transitions from a particular category.

For quick access to any transition, you can also type the name of a transition in the search box to the right of these drop-down menus, as seen in the illustrations on the following pages, and the transition will be brought to the top as you type.

Fade In and Fade Out

Fades, in and out of a clip, are most easily achieved by right-clicking on a clip on your timeline or sceneline and selecting the Fade In or Fade Out option.

This works for audio as well as video clips. Right-clicking on a clip which includes both audio and video, you'll find separate Fade In and Fade Out options for both the clip's audio and its video.

A fade in or fade out can be easily added to any video or audio clip by simply right-clicking on it and selecting the option from the pop-up menu

Video Transitions

Video Transitions are displayed in the Transitions panel as thumbnails representing their effect. If you click or hover your mouse over any thumbnail, you will see an animated representation of the Transition in action.

The categories of Transitions are:

3-D Motion – These transitions give the illusion that your video images are turning or flipping in three-dimensional space.

Dissolve – **Cross-Dissolve** is the most basic transition, a fade from one clip to the next. The **Dip to Black** transition fades the first clip to black before fading the next clip up from black.

GPU Transitions – These transitions include more advanced transitions, such as **Page Curl** and **Page Roll**. You will only see these transitions listed in the panel, however, if your computer's graphics card supports GPU effects.

Iris – Iris transitions change from one clip to another through a shape.

Map – These transitions map the transitional phase to your clip's luminance values.

NewBlue 3D Explosions, NewBlue 3D Transformations, NewBlue Art Blends, NewBlue Motion Blends – These categories contain very cool effects created by NewBlue, one of the world's top video effects companies.

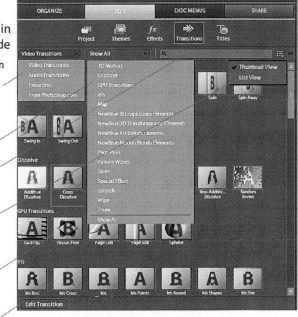

The Transitions panel in Video Transitions mode

The Transitions drop-down menu offers access to the other Transitions sets

The categories filter drop-down gives you quick access to any category of transitions

Quickly call up any transition by typing its name in the search box

Display transitions by thumbnail or list

Hover your mouse over any thumbnail to preview the transition

After transition is applied click Edit Transition to adjust it in the Properties panel

To apply a transition, drag it between two clips on your project's timeline or sceneline

Page Peel – These transitions give the illusion of a page peeling or rolling away between clips.

Slide – Slide transitions seem to push one clip out of the way for another or reveal it through sliding boxes or swirls.

Picture Wipes – These transitions use graphics (stars, travel signs, wedding dress lace) to transition from one clip to another.

Special Effects – A hodge podge of very showy transitions.

Stretch – These transitions seem to twist or stretch one clip away to reveal another.

Wipe – A variety of transitions that replace one clip with another with a clear line of movement. (See **Gradient Wipe** below for more information on this unique transition.)

Zoom – High energy transitions that suddenly shrink or enlarge one clip to reveal another.

The Transitions panel in
Audio Transitions mode

The Transitions drop-down
menu offers access to
the other Transitions sets

There are only two audio
transitions, subtly
different audio crossfades

After transition is applied
click Edit Transition to
adjust it in the Properties panel

To apply a transition, drag it between two clips
on your project's timeline or sceneline

Audio Transitions

To display the Audio Transitions, select Audio Transitions from
the Transitions panel's drop-down menu.

There are only two Audio Transitions, **Constant Gain** and
Constant Power, both variations of an audio cross-fade. The
difference between the two is minor, having to do with whether
the effect transitions from one audio clip to another in a linear
fashion or by varying the audio levels as they crossfade. Of the
two, Constant Power is generally considered to provide the
smoother transitional sound.

Adding Transitions

Adding a transition to your Premiere Elements project is as
simple as dragging it from the Transitions panel to the point
where two clips meet on your timeline or sceneline. In Sceneline
mode, there is even a placeholder in which to drag the transition
between the clips. In Timeline mode, you drag the transition
onto a spot where two clips meet. The transition you've added
between two clips is represented by a purple arrow graphic
overlapping one or both of the clips. (See **How Transition
Work**, below, for information on why transitions position
themselves where they do on your clips.)

If you'd like to increase or decrease the speed of a transition
on the timeline, you can do so my simply clicking on it and
dragging it wider. You can also change the transition's property,
as discussed below. Transitions, by defaults, are one second long.
However, you can make them as long or as short as you'd like.

Customizing a transition in the Properties panel

To open a transition's properties, double-click on it in your project's timeline or sceneline or click to select it and click Edit Transition in the Transitions panel

Each transition has its own set of customizable properties, but virtually all include the options to set where the transition centers and how long the transition lasts as well as the option to reverse the transition's animation

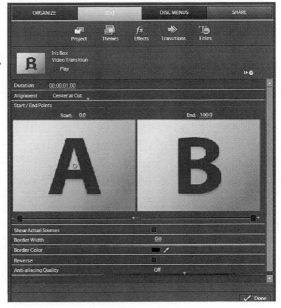

Once you've placed a transition, you can also customize it. Right-click on the transition on your timeline or sceneline and select Show Properties or simply double-click on it to open it in the Properties panel.

At the very least, you'll have a couple of basic customization options available in the Properties panel. Some transitions have several. You may need to scroll down in the panel to see all of the options available.

At Alignment, you can select whether the transition overlaps one or the other or both clips evenly.

You can check the option to reverse the transition so that, for instance, it replaces the old clip with the new from left to right rather than right to left.

Many transitions include other options, and you can preview the transition, even with the actual source clips (Check the Show Actual Sources box), right there in the Properties panel before you commit.

To create the transitional sequence, the transition must "borrow" extra footage – from beyond the out point of clip 1 and from beyond the in point of clip 2, sometimes resulting in the transition showing trimmed footage.

Out point of clip 1

"Head material" beyond in point of clip 1

Transition

In point of clip 2

"Tail material" beyond the out point of clip 2

How Transitions Work

Sometimes transitions seem to be behaving in mysterious ways. However, once you understand what's actually going it, you may find it easier to work with the process.

In order to create the transitional segment, during which both clips are displayed, the transition that you add needs to add a few extra frames, beyond one clip's end and the next clip's beginning. Officially these extra frames are called "head" and "tail" material. Unfortunately, this sometimes means that frames you've trimmed away from the end or beginning of a clip will appear during this transitional segment!

If this happens, you may need to trim a few more frames from the beginning or end of the clip so that, even amidst the transition, these frames are not displayed.

If there are no extra frames beyond the beginning or end of the clips you're transitioning, the program will create a freeze frame of the last available video frame for the clip and use that for the transitional material. This, too, can be a bit annoying if you're not aware of why it's happening. Once again, the solution is to trim back the clip so that the transition has some extra "head" or "tail" material to work with.

You may also find, sometimes, that the transition will not sit evenly between two clips on your timeline but seems to be entirely over one or the other clip. This is because the transition was not able to find the necessary head or tail material on at least one of the clips, and so it is building the transitional segment using "live" material from one clip and head or tail material from the other. If this is not what you want, you can enter the transitions Properties panel, as described above, and force it to sit evenly over both clips. However, you may find that this also creates an undesirable effect (such as a freeze frame in the head or tail material). So weigh your options carefully. The default point at which the transition lands is usually the best available position for it.

If you're using transitions between several photos (as in a slideshow) or even titles, you may find that the transition seems to be resting over one or the other clip entirely. In this case, it's best not to bother to tweak its position since, with a still image, head, tail and freeze frames all look the same.

The Gradient Wipe

One of the most versatile Video Transitions available in Premiere Elements 7 is the Gradient Wipe. The Gradient Wipe will create a custom wipe from one clip to another based on any gradient (black to gray to white) pattern you provide. By using custom patterns you've designed, you can create almost any kind of wipe pattern you can imagine!

Once you drag the Gradient Wipe onto a point between two clips, open the Properties panel, as described in **Adding**

The Gradient Wipe transition creates a wipe in any shape you create, by following the pattern from black to white.

To load a custom pattern, click the Custom button in the transition's Properties panel, then click Select Image in the Gradient Wipe Settings and browse to your image.

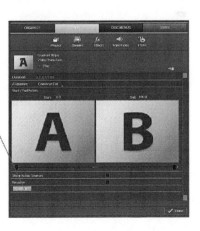

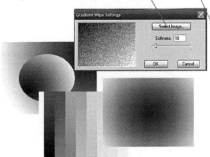

Transitions above, either by right-clicking on the transition on your timeline or sceneline and selecting Show Properties or by double-clicking on the transition.

At the bottom of the options listing for the Gradient Wipe in the Properties panel, you'll see a button labeled Custom. Click on this button to open the Gradient Wipe Settings panel. This panel will display a default gradient pattern along with a slider to adjust its softness.

Click on Select Image, however, and you'll be able to browse to any gradient image on your computer – or any photo or graphics file at all, in fact – and select it for a pattern for the wipe. The Gradient Wipe will base its wipe pattern on a movement from the blackest to the whitest area in the graphics file or pattern you've provided.

For more information on the Gradient Wipe and how to use it – plus a free pack of several gradient patterns – see my *Steve's Tips* article "The Gradient Wipe" and the free "mi – Gradient Wipe Pack" on the products page at Muvipix.com.

The Default Transition

If you ever use the Create Slideshow feature in Premiere Elements (see **Create Slideshow** in **Chapter 6: The Project Media Panel**) you'll note that it offers you the option of applying the Default Transition between all of your slides. By default, that transition is Cross-Dissolve. However, you can easily designate any transition in the Transition panel as the Default Transition.

To designate a transition as your default, right-click on the selected transition in the Transitions panel and select the Set Selected as Default Transition option.

Chapter 10

Titles
Creating text and titles for your project

There are actually two different routes to the Titles panel and workspace. One path gets you directly there; The other takes you to the workspace by way of a Title Templates panel.

To go directly to the Titles workspace, click on the "T" icon on the toolbar that runs along the bottom of the Monitor panel.

To go to the Titles workspace by way of the Title Templates panel, click on the Edit tab on the Tasks panel and select Titles. Once you've selected and applied a template in this workspace, you'll be taken to the Titles workspace.

Whichever route you take, once you select a template or enter the Titles workspace, a title clip will automatically be added to your project's timeline or sceneline. In Timeline mode, you will be able to see the clip on your project's timeline, on the lowest video track with no other clips on it except titles, and you can trim its duration or reposition it as you would any other still clip. (See **Trimming and Slicing** in **Chapter 11: The Timeline/Sceneline Panel.**) In Sceneline mode, you will only be able to see the title clip if it has been added to a movie in a space with no other video. Otherwise, it will be displayed in the Monitor and will be indicated with a small icon in the upper right corner of your clip's thumbnail on the sceneline.

Title Templates
Clicking the Titles button under the Edit tab in the Tasks panel displays a library of title templates, each shown as a thumbnail. (Black areas in the thumbnail usually represent transparency, through which your main or background video will be displayed.)

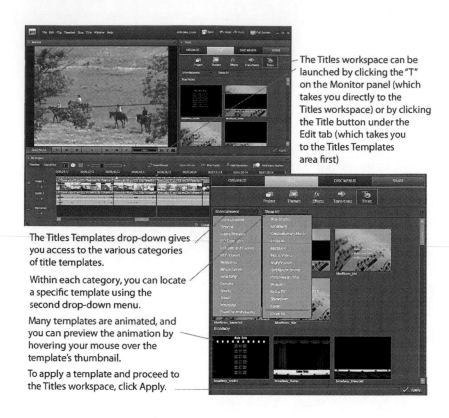

The Titles workspace can be launched by clicking the "T" on the Monitor panel (which takes you directly to the Titles workspace) or by clicking the Title button under the Edit tab (which takes you to the Titles Templates area first)

The Titles Templates drop-down gives you access to the various categories of title templates.

Within each category, you can locate a specific template using the second drop-down menu.

Many templates are animated, and you can preview the animation by hovering your mouse over the template's thumbnail.

To apply a template and proceed to the Titles workspace, click Apply.

Using the drop-down menus, as in the illustration above, you can isolate your templates by category or select a specific template. You also have the option of downloading additional materials from Photoshop.com

The templates usually include a graphic design and placeholders for adding your custom text.

Once you've clicked on a template to select, click the Apply button in the lower right corner of the panel. The title template will be applied, the title will appear on your timeline or sceneline and you'll move into the Titles workspace.

The Titles Workspace

The Titles workspace is loaded with tools for creating and customizing your project's titles. When you enter this

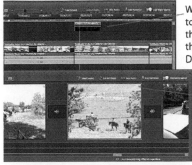

When you create a title it is automatically added to your movie project. In Timeline mode, the title will appear on the lowest available video track. Double-click it to launch the Titles workspace for re-editing.

In Sceneline mode, if overlayed on video, the title will be indicated by an icon in the upper right corner of the thumbnail

To duplicate a title in order to reuse the style and layout, right-click on the title in your Project media panel and select Duplicate. Don't use Copy/Paste or you'll merely clone the title, and any changes will apply to both titles.

workspace, a title clip is automatically added to your timeline or sceneline at the point of the CTI (Current Time Indicator).

If you've come to the Title workspace directly, by clicking on the "T" icon on the toolbar along the bottom of the Monitor panel, the words "Add Text" will be displayed in the Monitor. This placeholder text will be already selected when you launch this workspace and, when you start typing, your new text will replace it.

If you've come to this workspace by way of the Title Templates workspace, your title is already well underway, and you can click on any of the placeholder text boxes and type to replace the text there with your own. You can also move and remove any of the text or graphics on the template by selecting the Selection Tool (the arrow) from the Titles Toolbar (as described below), then clicking to select the element or text box and dragging it to a new location or removing it by pressing the Delete key.

If you haven't turned on the Safe Margins on the Monitor, make sure you do so before building your titles. To do this, click on the >> button in the upper right corner of the Monitor panel and check the option for Safe Title Margin. (If the >> button isn't visible, go to the Window drop-down and select Show Docking Headers.) The Safe Title Margin (the inner rectangle of two sets of rectangular guides that are displayed on your Monitor) won't show up on your final video output.

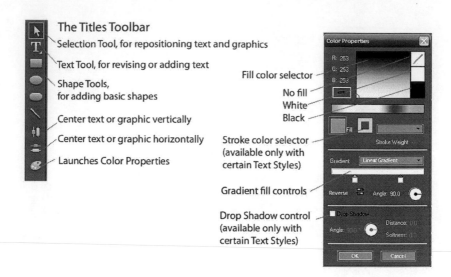

It's purpose is to offer a guide to protect you from TV screens that cut off some of the edge from your video image (quite common). Keeping all of your onscreen text within the bounds of the inner Safe Title Margin ensures that it will always be displayed completely, with no chance of any accidental cut-off.

The Toolbar
The Title Toolbar is displayed along the right side of the Monitor in the Title Workspace. The tools include:

The Selection Tool (the arrow) – Clicking the Selection Tool allows you to use your mouse cursor to drag the text blocks and graphic elements to new positions on your title.

The Text Tool (the "T") – The Text Tool changes the mode of your cursor to a text editor. If you click on an existing text box on your title, you will be able to edit the text; if you click any place else on your title, you will create a new text box on the same title into which you can add more text.

The Shape Tools (the rectangle, the oval, the rounded oval, the line) – Selecting the Shape Tools allows you to draw basic geometric shapes on your title by clicking and dragging. You can recolor these shapes by clicking to select them and then using the Color Properties tool, as described below.

The Center Vertical and **Center Horizontal Tools** – If you've selected a text box or graphic element on your title using the Selection Tool (above), clicking on either of these center tools centers it in your video frame.

Color Properties (the artist's palette) – After you've dragged over text to select it or used the Selection Tool (above) to select a text box or shape, you can recolor it by clicking on this icon. On the Color Properties panel that opens, **Fill** is the color of the shape or text itself, **Stroke** is the outline around it. The **Stroke Weight** is how thick the outline is. A **Gradient** is a blend from one color to another. Clicking the **Drop Shadow** option creates a shadow below your text or graphic. The characteristics of the gradient and the drop-shadow can be customized with the various settings.

Fill, Gradient and Drop Shadow can be applied to any shapes drawn with the Shape Tool.

Fill, Gradient and Drop Shadow can be applied also to any text. However, in order to apply a Stroke to the text, you must have selected a stroked Text Style, as described below.

Rolling and Crawling Titles

Any titles you create can automatically be made to roll (go up over the video frame) or crawl (move across a video frame). To access the Roll/Crawl Options screen, select Roll/Crawl Options from the >> button on the upper right corner of the Monitor panel. (If this button isn't visible, select Show Docking Headers from the Window drop-down menu.) This option screen can also be launched by clicking on the Roll/Crawl Options icon in the lower left corner of the Tasks panel.

The options on this screen are fairly intuitive. If you select Crawl, for instance, you have the option of setting it to either Crawl Left or Crawl Right across the video frame.

The Timing options allow you to set the roll or crawl to start and/or end off screen. If you set it to start or end off screen, you can set a Preroll or Postroll time for how long the title is off the screen. The Ease In and Ease Out options allow you to

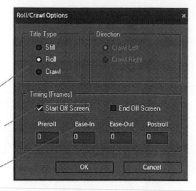

Roll/Crawl Options can be accessed from the >> button in the top right of theTitles monitor panel or from the button in the lower left corner of the Titles workspace panel

Crawls move horizontally across the screen, Rolls move up from the bottom of the screen

Options for starting or ending the title off the screen

Ease In and Ease Out slow the title at the beginning or end of the roll or crawl

change the rolling or crawling movement from a steady speed to one that begins slow and speeds up (Ease In) or vice versa (Ease Out).

The speed at which the title rolls or crawls is determined by how long the title is. Dragging out one end of the title on your timeline to increase its duration slows the speed of the roll or crawl; Dragging in an end of the title in to decrease its duration increases the speed of the roll or crawl. (Duration is a function of Timeline mode rather than Sceneline mode.)

As an alternative to using these automatic roll and crawl options, you can keyframe the movement of your title so that it is revealed through any movement or effect you can imagine. To learn more about using keyframing, see **Chapter 13: Keyframing.**

Adding a Graphic

To add a graphic or any image or photo from your computer to your title, click the Add Image icon in the lower left of the Tasks panel and browse to the picture file. Once you've added the graphic, use the Selection Tool to size and position it on your video frame. (See **The Toolbar,** above.)

The Titles Panel

While in the Titles workspace, the Tasks panel displays a number of options for stylizing your title's text. Drag over your

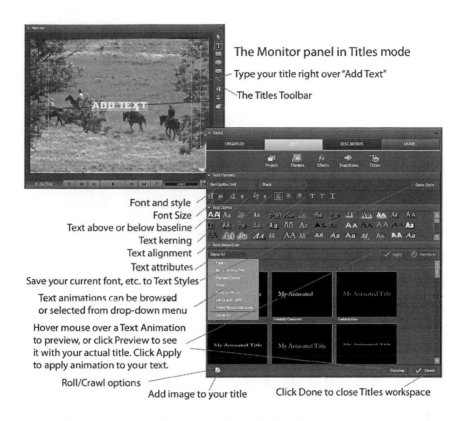

The Monitor panel in Titles mode

Type your title right over "Add Text"

The Titles Toolbar

Font and style
Font Size
Text above or below baseline
Text kerning
Text alignment
Text attributes
Save your current font, etc. to Text Styles

Text animations can be browsed
or selected from drop-down menu

Hover mouse over a Text Animation
to preview, or click Preview to see
it with your actual title. Click Apply
to apply animation to your text.

Roll/Crawl options

Add image to your title

Click Done to close Titles workspace

text to select it or use the Selection Tool (see **The Toolbar**, above) and click to select a text box in order to apply these options to it.

Text Options

The basic options for your title's text are Font, Size, Baseline Shift (raising or lowering the selected text relative to the unselected text), Left Align/Center/Right Align and Font Style.

Once you've applied these settings to your selected text and colored it (using the Color Properties on the Toolbar, described in **The Toolbar**, above), you can then save it as a permanent style in your Text Styles menu (discussed below). With the styled text selected, click the Save Style button and then name the style. It will then appear as an "Aa" thumbnail among the other Text Styles.

Re-editing a Title

If, after you've created a title, you need to re-edit it, you can re-open that title's workspace by double-clicking the title on your project's timeline.

Text Styles

Text Styles are fonts, font styles and colors that can be applied to your selected text simply by clicking on the "Aa" thumbnail representing the style.

Some of the styles include outlined or "stroked" text. If you apply a Text Style that includes an outline, or "stroke," you will have the option to change the color and weight of the stroke in Color Properties (see **The Toolbar,** above).

If you right-click on any of these Text Styles in the Titles panel, you will find the option to set it as the Default Style. The Default Style is the font, color and font style that will appear whenever you create new text for your title and will appear as your default font and color whenever you create a new title.

Text Animations

A new feature in version 4, the Text Animations effects have been refined in version 7. Text Animations, as the name implies, are ways of animating how your title text is introduced onto or removed from your video frame. Again, remember that you must have the text or text block selected in order for these animations to be applied.

The Text Animations are in several categories, and you can filter the animations displayed in the panel by selecting a category from the drop-down menu that displays Show All be default.

To see a preview of how the animation looks, just hover your mouse over any of the animation thumbnails. (This is a pretty intensive function, and the performance of this feature, including previews, can be limited by your computer's RAM load and graphics card power.) You can also click to select an animation (with your text or text block also selected, of course) and click the Preview button at the bottom right of the panel to see a preview of your actual text with the text animation applied.

Once you've clicked to select a text animation, click the Done button. The program will be returned to the Edit workspace and your title, with any styles or animations you've applied, will appear on your timeline or sceneline at the position of the CTI (Current Time Indicator).

Duplicating a Title

If you like how your title looks and you want to use the look and style for another title, you can duplicate it and then edit the duplicate. To duplicate a title, right-click on it in the Project media panel (under the Edit tab) and select Duplicate. You can then drag the duplicate title to your timeline and double-click on it to re-open the title's workspace for editing.

It's important that you duplicate the title in the Project media panel rather than merely doing a copy-and-paste on the timeline. If you create a copy of the title rather than a duplicate, then you've merely created a clone, and any changes you make to one title will be made to both – and that's likely not how you intend to use the title's copy.

Saving a Tile

If you like your title's layout and would like to save it for use in other Premiere Elements projects, you can do so by clicking to select the title either on your project's timeline or in your Project media panel and, from the File drop-down menu at the top the interface, select Export, then Title.

To import this title into another Premiere Elements project, just browse to it using the PC Files and Folders option for Get Media. (See **Getting Media from PC Files and Folders** in **Chapter 3: Getting Media**.)

Rendering your title

Your title will likely look a bit rough when you first play it back from your timeline or sceneline. To get a better idea of what the segment will look like when you output your movie, press the Enter key to render your video. (For more information, see **Rendering** in **Chapter 11: The Timeline/Sceneline Panel**.)

Chapter 11

The Timeline/Sceneline Panel
Your video editing workspace

Although every panel in Premiere Elements 7 has its role in your editing workflow, the Timeline/Sceneline panel (or, as Adobe calls it, the **My Project** panel) is the arena where the real video editing action takes place. It's where your clips are gathered, ordered, trimmed, sliced, rearranged, effected and, in many cases, adjusted. It's where your clips interact with each other. In short, it's where you're movie is made.

Although there are benefits to either workspace in the Timeline/Sceneline panel, the Timeline mode is generally considered to be the superior of the two modes. Sceneline is great for quick and simple assembly of clips on a single track of video. But, if you really want to utilize the full power of this great little program, you'll want to work in the Timeline mode, as I hope the discussion below will make very clear.

Sceneline Mode
The Sceneline is a very simplified timeline. Clips you drop into it snap into video placeholders on a single video track, audio included. Transitions pop into the transitions placeholders. Additional audio is dragged to one of two additional audio tracks. (Although the icons to the left of each track seem to imply that one is for voice and the other is for music, you can use either on either track.)

The emphasis in Sceneline view is on the content rather than the timing of it. You can't easily trim your clips to fit with the rest of your movie's pacing and, if you add a Title, you can't easily access the Title or adjust its position, in time, relative to your video. In short, this is a drag-and-drop interface. Simple and, consequently, rather limited.

Emphasis on content

Single video track

Two audio tracks (in addition to clip audio)

Audio level adjusts for entire video track only

Sceneline Mode

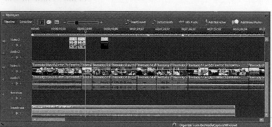

Emphasis on time and how clips interact with each other

Up to 99 video and audio tracks

Ability to trim and reposition clips relative to each other

Audio levels can be adjusted for precise moments

Timeline Mode

There is one advantage to this workspace, however, beyond its simplicity. If you click on the speaker icons to the left of the video track or either of the audio tracks, an audio level slider will appear. The slider allows you to raise or lower the volume for an entire audio track in a single move.

But there, too, your control is rather limited. In most cases you'll likely want to adjust your audio levels at specific points, not for an entire track for an entire movie. And that is something much more easily accomplished in Timeline mode.

The Timeline

Premiere Elements professional-style Timeline is one of the most powerful work areas in the program. The timeline can be expanded to accommodate a virtually unlimited number of audio and video tracks (officially 99 of each – though you'd need a pretty powerful computer to use that many at once).

The Video 1 track is paired with three audio tracks (Although they are labeled as Soundtrack, Narration and Audio 1, you can use any audio on any track). Additional video tracks will be paired with accompanying audio tracks, stacked above the basic set – although, if you plan to use a lot of video-only clips, you can save some space by turning off the audio tracks by unchecking the option, available by clicking the >> button in the upper right corner of the panel. (If the >> button is not visible, go to the Window drop-down menu and select Show Docking Headers.) Under this same >> menu, you can find options for adding tracks or changing the track heights.

The timeline in Premiere Elements is set to "ripple" as you add and remove clips from your project. This means that the program snaps your clips together and to the left whenever possible. Deleting a clip from your project will cause the other clips to the right to snap left to fill in the gap; inserting a clip within an assemblage of clips will cause all clips to the right to move right to accommodate it, splitting clips if you insert one clip mid-clip. If you insert a clip into a project with clips on parallel tracks, the program will split all of the video on all of the tracks to accommodate it.

In most cases, this will work to your advantage. If you've got a whole assemblage of audio and video clips in your movie and you decide to reorder it or add a clip to the middle of your project, you'll want the rest of the movie to stay together, moving aside to allow this inserted clip in.

But there also may be times when you'll want to override this ripple function – as when you've assembled a movie and you're trying to add background music to it. By default, the program will assume you're trying to *insert* this music clip into the midst of your movie. And, when you add the music, the program will split your movie and slide all of the other clips aside.

However, **holding down the Ctrl key** as you add your new clip will override this ripple function. The rest of your clips will hold their positions, and you'll be able to place your music on an audio track – or any clip on any audio or video track – without disturbing the rest of your movie.

Particularly if you're doing multi-track editing, holding down this Ctrl key is just about the only way to keep your movie clips in place as you continually add and remove clips on other tracks.

Zooming In

You can zoom into the clips on your timeline, close enough to trim the individual frames from your clips if you'd like, or zoom out wide enough to see your entire project on the timeline and beyond.

To add a clip to your timeline or sceneline, simply drag it from the Project media panel.

In Timeline mode, the other clips will "ripple", moving aside if you add the clip in the middle of a project.

To override the ripple effect (as when you're adding music or a video clip to a parallel track) hold down the Ctrl key as you add the clip.

Zoom in or out on the timeline by pressing + or - or using the Zoom slider.

To zoom out press the − key on your keyboard and to zoom in press the + key, or drag the slider in the center top of the Timeline panel toward − or +. To snap to a view of your entire project on the timeline at once, press the \ key.

Adding Clips to the Timeline or Sceneline

Adding clips to your project's timelineor sceneline is about as intuitive as it can be. Simply drag the clips from the Organizer (Organizer tab, Organizer) or your Project's media panel (Edit tab, Project). You can reorder the clips on the timeline or sceneline simply by dragging them around. Placing a clip to the left of another clip will force it to slide aside to accommodate the move.

To delete a clip from your timeline or sceneline, click to select it and press the Delete button on your keyboard or right-click on it and select **Delete**. Unless there are clips on parallel video or audio tracks, the timeline will ripple to fill in the gap.

To remove clip without causing the other clips to ripple or fill in the gap, right-click on the clip and select **Clear** instead.

Once your clips are assembled, you can apply transitions between them simply by dragging a transition from the Transitions panel. More information on this feature can be found in **Chapter 9: The Transitions Panel**.

Trimming and Slicing

Once your clip is on your timeline, you can trim it to remove unwanted portions. To do so, click to select the clip and hover your mouse over the clip's end. When your mouse's cursor indicates that it's in trim mode (It will become a ⊒⊶ or a ⊶⊑ cursor), then click and drag the end of the clip. The Monitor will preview the new in or out point as you drag. (For information on pre-trimming your clip before you drag it to the timeline or sceneline, see **The Clip Monitor** in **Chapter 6: The Project Panel**.)

To slice a clip – either to remove a portion of it or to isolate a segment so that you can add an effect to it – position the CTI (Current Time Indicator) at the position on the timeline you'd like to slice and click the Scissors icon in the Monitor panel.

If you have a clip selected on your timeline, this tool will slice only that clip; if you have no clips selected, the tool will slice through all of the clips on all tracks at the CTI's current position.

If you then want to delete a segment you've sliced (or sliced on either side of), click to select the segment, right-click and choose Delete or Clear, depending on how you'd like the timeline to behave.

If you find, after removing a segment, that you've removed too much of a clip – or not enough – you can simply drag an end of the clip to re-trim it and replace or remove the extra frames.

To slice a clip in two, click the Slice (scissors) tool on the Monitor panel.

If a clip is selected on the timeline, only that clip will be split at the position of the CTI; If no clips are selected, all clips on every track on the timeline will be split at the position of the CTI.

⊶⊑ Trim from Beginning of clip   Trim from End of clip ⊒⊶

To trim a clip on the timeline, hover your mouse over the beginning or end of clip until the Trim from Beginning or Trim from End icons appears, then click and drag in or out.

Still Photos

Still photos are dragged to the timeline or sceneline just as video clips are. By default, the duration of a still photo in a Premiere Elements project is five seconds. (This default can be changed under Edit/Preferences – although changing it will only affect photos brought into the program *after* the preference has been changed.)

You can increase or decrease how long the photo displays on the timeline by dragging to trim or extend it, the same way you would trim or extend any clip, as described above.

As explained in **Working With Photos** in **Chapter 3: Getting Media**, you'll get the best performance from stills if they are sized to no larger than 1000x750 pixels. Additionally, once you've placed a photo on your timeline, you can eliminate a somewhat common problem (related to interlacing) by right-clicking on the still on the timeline and selecting Field Options and then selecting the **Flicker Removal** option. Applying this setting will preempt a fluttering problem that sometimes manifests itself in video outputs when highly detailed or high contrast photos are used in Premiere Elements projects.

Creating audio only or video only clips

There are times you want to use only the video of a clip without the audio. There are also times when you want the audio from a clip but not the video.

Deleting one or the other from a clip on the timeline is as simple as right-clicking on the clip and selecting either Delete Audio or Delete Video from the right-click menu.

Fading in and fading out

The simplest way to fade into or out of a clip is to right-click on it and select Fade In or Fade Out from the right-click menu. (Separate options are offered for fading in or out your video and your audio, if your clip includes both.)

By default, your fades will last one second. You can, however, adjust the keyframe positions to lengthen or shorten that time. To do this, look for the white dot that Premiere Elements has placed to create the fade on the thin, horizontal, yellow line

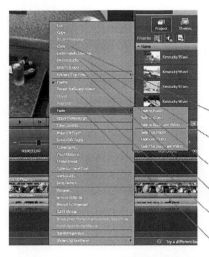

**Right-click options for clips
on your timeline**

Clear clip and do not ripple gap closed

Delete clip and ripple gap closed

Remove audio from your clip

Remove video from your clip

Unlink audio and video

Fade In/Out options for your clips

that runs through your clip. That dot is called a keyframe, and we discuss it in much greater detail in **Chapter 13: Keyframing**. By default, that yellow line represents Opacity on your video clips and Volume on your audio. See how the line slants down before or after that keyframe? That's your fade in or fade out.

Adjusting that dot's position relative to the end of the clip by clicking on it and dragging it extends or shortens the duration of your fade in or fade out. To find out more about adjusting your audio's volume and how to control it as specific points in your movie, see **Adjusting Audio Levels on the Timeline,** below.

L-cuts, J-cuts and Multiple Tracks
The ability to compose your video using several audio and video tracks greatly expands the opportunities you have to do interesting and professional-style things with your movie.

Multiples tracks of audio, of course, merely mix into a single soundtrack for your movie. (See **Mix Audio**, below.) With multiple tracks of video, on the other hand, you can combine elements of several video clips at once using a variety of properties and effects.

Using Scaling and Position settings with multiple tracks of video allows for Picture-in-Picture effects well as the opportunity to do split screens, showing several video clips on screen at once

Think of multiple tracks of video as a stack. In most cases, only the uppermost track in the stack will be visible. However, if you change the scale and position of the clips on the uppermost track – or on several tracks – you can display several tracks at once. (This Picture-in-Picture effect can be achieved using **Presets**, as discussed in **Chapter 8: The Effects Panel**, or by adjusting their Scale and Position, as discussed in **Chapter 12: The Properties Panel**.)

You can also reveal portions of clips on lower tracks by using effects such as **Chroma Key** (as discussed in **Chapter 8: The Effects Panel**), any of the Matte effects or even the Crop effect. By keyframing these Properties, you can make these positions, sizings or other settings change over the duration of the clip. (For more information, **Chapter 13: Keyframing**.)

Using multiples tracks of video and then scaling and positioning your clips on each, you can have any number of video images in your video frame at the same time. (Think the grid of faces in the opening credits of *The Brady Bunch*.) The products page at Muvipix.com offers a wealth of tutorials describing techniques for achieving these effects.

Addiitionally, two popular techniques that use multiple tracks of video are the **L-cut** and the **J-cut,** so named because, back in the days of single-track editing, when a segment of video had to be removed and the audio left in place to allow for the placement of alternate video, the primary video and audio clip resembled an L or a J (depending on which segment was removed).

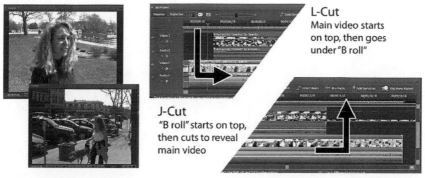

L-Cut
Main video starts on top, then goes under "B roll"

J-Cut
"B roll" starts on top, then cuts to reveal main video

As audio from main clip continues, video cuts to or from "B roll" footage.

Consider a TV news report that features video of a reporter shown standing in front of a burned-out building, describing the fire that destroyed it. As he continues speaking, the video cuts away to footage shot earlier of the fire itself. That's an L-cut. (A J-cut, on the other hand, begins with the cut-away video and the reporter's voice heard on the soundtrack, then cuts back to the reporter finishing his report.)

Creating an L-cut is easy with multi-track editing. Put the main video, the clip of the reporter speaking to the camera, (we'll call it Clip A) on Video track 1. Then, holding the Ctrl key to override the timeline's ripple function, place the secondary video, the old footage of the fire, (Clip B) on Video track 2, overlapping the latter part of Clip A, as seen above. (Right-click on Clip B and select Delete Audio, if necessary.) Voila! Tweak Clip B's position for maximum effect and you're done! We begin with the reporter speaking to the camera and, as he continues to speak, we cut away to the footage of the fire.

L-cuts and J-cuts are very effective for news-style reports as well as for interviews, in which you cut away to separately shot footage or even a slideshow of what the interviewee is describing. It's a great way to reinforce, with images, what's being presented verbally.

By the way, here's some professional vocabulary to impress your friends with. That secondary footage that plays as the main video's audio continues? It's commonly called "**B-roll footage**", a relic of the days when this kind of editing actually did involve cutting in footage from a separate roll of film or video.

The Work Area Bar can be set to designate only a portion of
your video project. Most Share options allow you to output the Work Area Bar segment only.

The Work Area Bar

The Work Area Bar is the lighter gray bar that runs below the
tick marks and numbers, along the top of the timeline. Usually,
this bar grows and shrinks with your project as you edit it but,
by dragging its beginning and end handles, you can manually
set it to cover only a portion of your video editing project.

Nearly all of the output option under Share include the
checkbox option **Export Work Area Bar Only.** Checking
this option directs the program to output only the segment of
your project you've defined with the Work Area Bar. For more
information on this function, see the discussions under each
output option in **Chapter 15: Share**.

To reset the bar over your project's entire active timeline, press
the \ key and then double-click the Work Area Bar.

Rendering

Premiere Elements uses a DV-AVI workflow. That means
that, whatever video or photos you put in, Premiere Elements
assimilates it and eventually re-renders it as a DV-AVI video
file before it outputs it as another video format. And that's true
even if you put an MPEG in and then output an MPEG from
the project you've created with it. Everything goes through
the process of becoming a DV-AVI before Premiere Elements
encodes it as anything else. This is why a project that is made
up of non-DV-AVI files can take much longer to transcode to a
DVD than one that is purely DV.

The Premiere Elements process of creating DV-AVI video from
non-DV-AVI source files is called rendering. Photos, MPEGs,
MOVs and VOBs must all be rendered by the program.

Additionally, the program must render DV-AVIs to which effects or transitions have been added.

When you use a non-DV-AVI video source, or apply an effect, title or transition to a DV-AVI source file, a red line will appear above the clip on your project timeline. This line indicates that the video you'll see, if you play back that particular video clip is a "soft render" – Premiere Elements is creating the preview video on the fly, as you play it. And, depending on what the video clip is, how many effects have been applied and how fast your computer system is, this playback can look pretty bad. Fuzzy. Low resolution. It may even have problems playing evenly.

If you render the clip, however, (just press the **Enter** key), the program will create a "hard render," a temp file of DV-AVI video that will show you what your video will actually look like when you do a final output. The red line above the clip will turn green and your playback will be much cleaner and smoother.

(DV-AVIs don't need to be rendered at all, and there will be neither a red nor green line above them on your timeline.)

You can render your clips as you're working. Or you can wait until your playback performance gets really bad. It's up to you. But do be aware that, if you're having playback problems and your Timeline has a lot of red lines running across the top, a few seconds of rendering can make things work much more smoothly again.

Adjusting Audio Levels on the Timeline

The audio level of the clips on your timeline is represented by a thin, horizontal, yellow line that runs through your clips. You can easily raise or lower the volume level for a clip by dragging that line higher or lower. (See also **Mix Audio**, below.)

But what about if you want to raise or lower the audio levels for a clip at specific points? Say you want to fade your music down for a few seconds so that your narration track can dominate? Or you have a conversation recorded in which one person speaks very quietly and you need to raise the audio level for his part of your clip while leaving the other half of recorded conversation as is? That's when you use keyframes. (For a more detailed discussion this feature, see **Chapter 13: Keyframing**.)

Audio keyframes can be used to adjust audio levels for specific points

When clip is selected (clicked on) audio keyframes can be added with the timeline's Add/Remove Keyframe button

Keyframes are added at the position of the CTI but can be dragged to any position

Dragging keyframes higher raises the clip's audio level; dragging lower reduces audio level

Dragging yellow line with no keyframes raises or lower audio level for entire clip

Audio keyframes are also easily added and adjusted right on your project's timeline. To create a keyframe point on your audio clip, click to select an audio or audio/video clip on your timeline and position the CTI (Current Time Indicator) over the approximate spot you want to add a keyframe to. (A clip must be selected and the CTI positioned over it in order to create a keyframe on the timeline.) Then click on the little, diamond-shaped Make Keyframe button on the left side of the timeline panel, left of the audio track. This will create a keyframe point, which will appear as a white dot on your audio clip at the position of the CTI. You can drag this dot to any position on the clip or change or delete it at any time.

Normalize: A great audio tool

One other audio tool that merits mentioning is the Normalize tool. Although it will override any other adjustments you've made to your clip's audio volume, it's a powerful and easy to use way to bring up or down the audio level for a entire clip with just a couple of clicks of the mouse.

To use it, merely right-click on your audio clip, select Audio Gain from the right-click menu and then click the Normalize button on the option screen. The tool will automatically analyze your clip and optimize the audio level for that clip, raising it as much as necessary to create a full sound.

Because it sets levels based on the loudest sound on the clip and affects the entire clip equally, it's not the perfect solution in every case. But it is a great quick fix for improving a clip with a low but even audio level.

Positioning the keyframe higher on the clip increases the volume at that point. Lowering it decreases the volume.

You can create as many keyframes as you need and use several to set the audio level higher for some segments and lower it for other segments on your clips. It's a valuable tool for evening out and controlling the sound in your video project.

Tools on the Timeline

In addition to its editing functions, Premiere Elements' Timeline and Sceneline panels offer a number of easy-to-access tools, represented by icons spread along the top of the panel.

Time Stretch (the clock icon)

Time Stretch is a very intuitive tool for speeding up or slowing down a clip. To use it, click on the clock icon and then select a clip and drag an end to lengthen or shorten it (in the same way we describe in **Trimming and Slicing**, above). Extending the duration of a clip slows it down. Shortening a clip speeds it up. (You can also set the playback speed of a clip manually by right-clicking on the clip on the Timeline and selecting **Time Stretch**, then setting the playback speed numerically.)

Properties (the list icon)

The Properties panel is one of the most powerful workspaces in the program. (For more information, see **Chapter 12: The Properties Panel**.) With the Properties panel open, click to select any clip on the timeline or sceneline. Its properties and effects will be listed in the panel and can be adjusted or removed. (This panel can also be accessed by right-clicking on a clip on the timeline and selecting **Show Properties**.)

Tools right on the Timeline and Sceneline panel

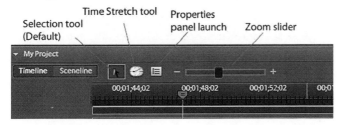

105

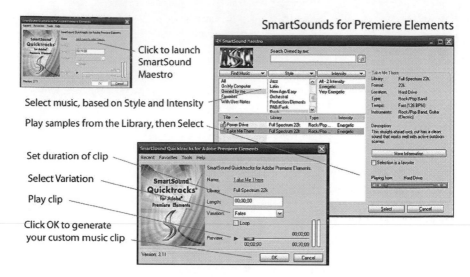

SmartSounds for Premiere Elements

Click to launch
SmartSound
Maestro

Select music, based on Style and Intensity

Play samples from the Library, then Select

Set duration of clip

Select Variation

Play clip

Click OK to generate
your custom music clip

SmartSound

SmartSound is a terrific, new, third-party feature that's been added in version 7. This amazing little program will create custom, professional-style music tracks, based on criteria you select, at whatever time duration you require.

To use it, click the SmartSound button on the Timeline/Sceneline panel. (Because it's a third-party program, you'll need to accept the licensing agreement and register the first time you use it.) At the Quicktracks splash screen that launches, click on the Click Here to Select Music link to open the SmartSound Maestro workspace.

The program offers a number of free music tracks. In the SmartSound Maestro, you'll find the complimentary tracks under the Find Music/On My Computer and Owned by Me selections. Select a Style and Intensity, then click to select a music track from the Library. Once you've done that, you can play a sample of the music using the player that will appear in the lower right of the interface.

Once you've selected your music, the real magic begins! You'll be returned to the SmartSound Quicktracks screen, where you can select a variation of your musical selection and set the exact length for the clip you want, which you can again preview. Then simply click OK and the program will custom create a rich, professional-style music track, precisely to your specifications. And, best of all, the track is royalty-free, so you can use it in any of your productions without restriction.

SmartSound also offers hundreds of musical clips and styles for purchase. (These are the clips you'll find if you select Find Music/All.) These can be purchased individually (for typically $14.95), or you can buy an entire package of similar music styles for $99. If you drop down the Find Music menu, you'll see SmartSound also offers a large number of sound effects for purchase.

Detect Beats

This cool tool can be used to create a slideshow that changes in rhythm with a music clip. To use the Detect Beats tool, select an audio clip on your timeline or sceneline and click on the Detect Beats icon. An option screen allows you to adjust the detection settings. The tool will then analyze your music clip and create unnumbered markers along the timeline to the beat of the song. (They'll look like little musical notes.)

Once these markers have been created, you can create a slideshow that automatically changes slides in time to the music. (You can learn more about this feature in **Create Slideshow** in **Chapter 6: The Project Panel**.)

The Detect Beats Tool

Click to select your musical clip on the timeline or sceneline, then click the Detect Beats button

Adjust settings as needed for your music

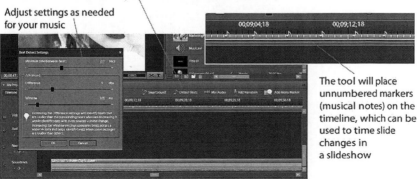

The tool will place unnumbered markers (musical notes) on the timeline, which can be used to time slide changes in a slideshow

Mix Audio

Clicking this button launches the Audio Mixer, a great panel to keep open as much as possible so that you can monitor your movie's audio levels, particularly as you begin the final phases of editing of your project.

The Audio Mixer displays the audio levels for each of your active audio tracks and offers controls for raising and lowering these audio levels. When you're not playing your video, you can click to select a clip on the timeline at the position of the CTI (Current Time Indicator) and the Audio Mixer sliders will raise and lower the volume level of the entire clip. If you adjust the sliders as your video is playing, keyframe points will be added to the clip so that the audio is raised or lowered only at the point at which you adjusted the slider.

As you play your project, watch the meters for each track, adjusting the sound levels as necessary to keep as much as possible in the green, with the bulk for audio peaking at zero or a little beyond. An occasional peak in the red will probably not cause problems, but too much will cause your video output to sound distorted.

In our opinion, this tool serves much more effectively as an audio meter than an audio level adjustment tool. If used to

The Audio Mixer will display separate controls for each audio track.

If adjustments are made while playback is stopped, adjustments will affect the entire clip. If made during playback, audio keyframes will be created.

adjust audio levels while the video is playing, it simply places too many hard-to-adjust audio keyframes on the timeline. You'll get much neater and much more effective results if you use the technique we describe in **Adjust Audio Levels on the Timeline**, above.

Add Narration

With this tool, you can easily add narration to your project, and even record it as you watch the video playing. To launch the Narration feature, click on the Add Narration button on your project's Timeline/Sceneline panel.

The Narration panel displays your microphone's recording level on the meter that runs along the left side panel. You'll want to keep it green and full, adjusting the slider as necessary for optimal sound. You can turn down your computer's speakers or select the option to Mute Audio While Recording so that you don't get feedback from the speakers as you record.

To start recording your narration, click the red Record button. The panel will display a three-second countdown and then will begin recording as your movie plays. Click the same button again to stop the recording.

The program will place the narration clip that you've recorded on the Narration audio track at the position of the CTI (Current Time Indicator) on your Timeline. The two shortcut buttons on the panel will jump you back to the beginning of

Add Narration panel

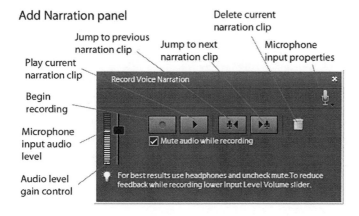

Delete current
narration clip

Jump to previous
narration clip

Jump to next
narration clip

Microphone
input properties

Play current
narration clip

Begin
recording

Microphone
input audio
level

Audio level
gain control

the clip you've just recorded (or to the next or previous narration clip). You can then click the play button to hear the results. If you're unhappy with it, you can click the shortcut button to jump back to the beginning of the clip and record new narration over it or, by clicking the trashcan icon, delete it completely.

A good microphone and sound card are essential to getting a good strong narration recording. If you're having problems getting the feature to work, double-check the audio settings in your computer to assure all is in order there (and ensure that your microphone isn't muted.).

Clicking on the microphone icon in the upper right corner of the Narration panel will display the name of the microphone or audio jack the Narration feature is configured for. If it's not correct, to go Premiere Elements' Edit drop-down menu and select Preferences/Audio Hardware. Click the ASIO Settings button, and adjust whatever settings are necessary there.

Finally, if you can't get the Narration feature to work at all in Premiere Elements, you can, as an alternative, record your narration into Windows Audio Recorder (usually under Accessories/Entertainment under your Start menu) and then import the audio clip into your project.

And I've found I get the best quality for my narration by just recording myself with my camcorder and then capturing Audio Only (as described in **Capturing MiniDV, HDV Video or Video from Webcams or WDM Devices** in **Chapter 3: Getting Media**.)

Add Menu Marker
The Add Menu Marker tool is a very important part of the DVD and BluRay disc authoring process. Menu Markers link to the disc menus you create as part of your disc authoring in Premiere Elements. (See **Chapter 14: Creating Disc Menus**.)

Clicking the Add Menu Marker icon creates a Menu Marker on your timeline or sceneline at the position of the CTI (Current Time Indicator). You can later drag the marker to any other position if you'd like.

Create Menu Marker Option Screen

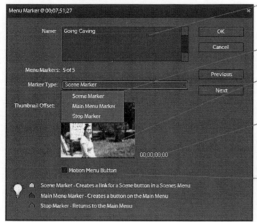

Name of scene as you'd like it to appear on your menu

Type of marker drop-down

Scene thumbnail that will appear on your menu

Option to set another frame in your video as your scene thumbnail

Option to make your thumbnail a video loop

When you create a new marker, the Menu Marker option screen opens. (You can reopen it at any time by double-clicking on the menu marker on the timeline or right-clicking on your clip on the sceneline and selecting the Set Menu Marker option.) This screen includes a number options for creating your marker.

There are three different types of Menu Markers, and you set which type of marker you've created in this option screen.

Green Scene Menu Markers will be to linked to your disc's scene menu.

Blue Main Menu Markers will be linked to your disc's main menu

Red Stop Markers stop your movie's playback and return your viewer to your disc's main menu. Using these Stop Markers, you can create a disc with a number of short movies on it, your viewer returning to the main menu at the end of each.

Type a name for your marker in the place provided. This name will automatically appear as the name of the link button on your disc's main or scene menu.

The image from your movie displayed in the Thumbnail Offset is what will appear as your menu button for this link. Changing the timecode by either typing in new numbers or clicking and dragging across the numbers will change which frame from your video is displayed as the button link. (However, changing this thumbnail image will not affect the location of the marker itself on your project's timeline.)

Clicking the Motion Menu Button checkbox will cause your link button to appear as a short video loop rather than a freeze frame.

For more information on how to create and use Menu Markers, see my *Steve's Tips* article "DVD Markers", available on the products page at Muvipix.com.

Chapter 12

The Properties Panel
Adjusting your effects settings

As you add effects to a clip, they are added to a list in that clip's Properties panel. You can launch the Properties panel workspace for a clip in a number of ways:

Click on the Properties button on the Timeline/Sceneline panel (the list icon, as indicated in the illustration on the following page); you'll need to then click on a clip on your sceneline or timeline to see its properties and effects;

Right-click on a clip on timeline or sceneline and select Show Properties;

Click to select a clip on your timeline or sceneline and, from the Effects panel, click the **Edit Effects button**; or

Select **Properties** from the Window drop-down menu

The Properties panel is second only to the Timeline/Sceneline panel as the most powerful and important workspace in the Premiere Elements. The Timeline/Sceneline panel may be where you assemble, trim and order your clips, but the Properties panel is where you make the movie magic happen!

It's where the effects are added, adjusted and removed, where motion paths are created, where many special effects are created.

Every clip has its own Properties panel, and when you select a clip and open the panel, you'll see the properties for that particular clip. When an effect is added to a clip, it is added to that clip's Properties list. It can then be adjusted, removed or keyframed in this panel.

Launching the
Properties panel

Select Properties from the
Window drop-down menu

Click Edit Effects in the
Effects panel

Click on the Properties
(list) icon on the timeline
or sceneline

Right-click on a clip on your
project's timeline or sceneline
and select Show Properties

Keyframing is the process of creating motion paths or effects
which change settings over time (such as a Crop effect with
the cropping in action or the Ripple effect that shows actual,
moving ripples across your clip). For a thorough discussion of
making magic by keyframing, see **Chapter 13: Keyframing**.

Default Clip Properties

There are some properties which are listed on every clip by
default. Which of these are included depends on whether the
clip is video only, audio only or both. To make an adjustment to
a property or effect, click on the little triangle to the left of the
property. This will open the property and display its individual
settings. (For more information on adjusting settings for effects,
see **Adjusting Effects** in **Chapter 8: The Effects Panel**.)

The default properties for every video or still clip are:

> **Image Control** – Includes the basic image adjustments of
> **Brightness, Contrast, Hue** (color, based on a 360 degree
> color wheel) and **Saturation** (density of color).

> **Motion** – Includes the properties of **Position, Scale** and
> **Rotation**, the settings used to keyframe motion paths. (See
> **Chapter 13: Keyframing** for detailed information on how

The Properties panel

The Properties panel lists all effects applied to a clip, including certain default properties.

Default video properties of Image Control Motion and Opacity

Default Audio properties of Volume and Balance

Click triangle to open settings for your effects and properties

Enable/disable effect or property

Reset selected effect to default

Loop audio playback for this clip

Play audio for this clip

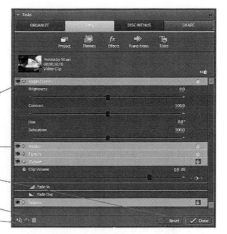

to create motion paths using this property.) Position is the position of the center of the clip in a video frame, measured in pixels. Scale is a percentage measurement for resizing of your video image. Rotation's setting is a measure of degrees of angle imposed on your video image. The settings for the Motion properties can easily be changed numerically or, more intuitively, by clicking on the video image in the Monitor panel and, dragging it or its corner angles to change its position, size or rotation.

Opacity – The of transparency level of a clip. (Well, technically opacity is the *non*-transparency level of a clip.) The fading in or out of a clip (Added to a video clip by right-clicking and selecting Fade in or Fade Out) is actually a function of opacity (revealing black as it is reduced) using keyframing to bring it from 0% opacity to 100% or vice versa.

The default properties for every audio clip are:

Volume – The raising and lowering of sound levels on an audio clip. This effect is one of the most common to keyframe, so that levels can be set differently for specific points on a clip. The easiest way to keyframe the audio settings is right on the Timeline (as discussed in **Adjusting Audio Levels on the Timeline** in **Chapter 11: The Timeline/Sceneline Panel**).

Balance – Balance effects the audio levels for left and right stereo sound channels relative to each other.

As effects are added to a clip, they are added to the list of Properties for the clip. Many effects can be added to a single clip, and you can even add multiples of the same effect to increase its intensity. This can be an effective way to raise the volume level of a clip with especially quiet audio; Continue to add Volume effects (See **Finding and Applying an Effect** in **Chapter 8: Effects**) and adjust the slider in the Properties panel to its maximum setting (see below) until the clip is at an acceptable level.

Many effects, when first applied, may not even show make a significant change in your clip at their default settings. And you may need to adjust the effects settings to see any real change.

Adjusting Settings for Effects and Properties

Once you're in the Properties panel, you'll see your applied effect listed along with the default clip properties (discussed above). Click the white triangle to the left of your effect to reveal its settings.

Some effects (such as Lightning) offer dozens of settings for customizing the effect. Others (such as Posterize) may offer only a few settings or even a single "intensity adjustment" slider.

Many effects (such Spherize, for instance) will show almost no change to your clip at their default settings. In nearly every case, once you've applied an effect to a clip, you'll need to change the settings to see any significant change to your audio or video. (Only a few Effects, such as the Black & White effect, have no settings at all – they're are either on or off.)

There are always several ways to adjust the settings for an effect.

Numerically – The numbers that represent an effect can, depending on the effect, represent the effects position (measured in pixels across the frame), percentage (as in opacity) or intensity. To change a number, you can click on it and type in a new amount or you can click over the number and drag right and left to increase or decrease the amount.

Adjusting effects
in the Properties panel

Open the effect's properties
to adjust using numbers or
the sliders

Settings vary with the
specifics of an effect

Many effects can be
adjusted by selecting
the effects listing for the
clip in the Properties
panel and dragging
the corner handles
in the Monitor display

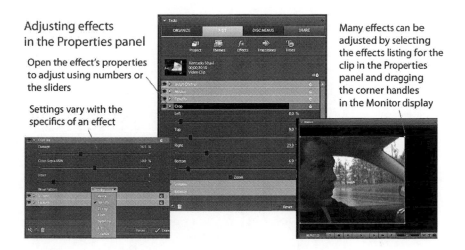

Sliders – The intensity or percentage for a large number
of effects settings can be increased or decreased simply by
moving its slider back and forth.

On the Monitor – The most intuitive way to adjust many
effects is to click to highlight the effect listing in the
Properties panel (corner handles will become active on
your video image) and then click on the video image in
the Monitor panel and drag it by its corner handles. For
effects that involve motion (such as repositioning, rotating
or resizing the video image) simply drag the image in the
monitor to a new position. For effects that involve shaping
or sizing (such as scaling, cropping or using one of the
garbage mattes) dragging the corner handles will reshape
the image or effected area.

Once you start adjusting the settings, the changes will be
immediately displayed in your Monitor panel. (If they're not,
it's because the CTI, or Current Time Indicator, on the timeline
isn't positioned over the clip you're adjusting.) The exception is
the Lightning effect, which is so intensive and erratic that you'll
need to play back the clip to see how your adjusted settings have
affected the clip.

Types of Effects Settings

Just as there is a wide variety of types of effects (some that shift colors, some that create transparency [see **Using Chroma Key** in **Chapter 8: Effects**], some that reshape or distort your video image), there is a wide variety of settings for these effects. Some settings increase the intensity of an effect. Some add optional elements to the effect. Other settings, depending on the effect, may shift color or define which areas on your video image are affected.

The Crop effect is an example. The settings for the crop effect define the percentage of the video image that will be cropped from each side. Dragging a slider representing any side's settings (or clicking to select the effect listing in the Properties panel and then dragging on the corner handles that become activated on the video image in the Monitor) trims back that side.

Additionally, any effect's settings can be set to change as the clip plays, creating an animated change, using keyframes. The Basic 3D effect, for instance, can be keyframed to create the illusion that your video image is tumbling back into space. The Crop effect can be keyframed so that the amount of the video image that is cut away changes over the course of the clip. For more information on how this amazing tool works, see **Chapter 13: Keyframing** .

Turning Effects On and Off and Removing Effects

Once you've adjusted the settings for an effect, you can easily do a before-and-after comparison by temporarily turning off or disabling the effect. To temporarily turn off the effect, click on the eyeball icon to the left of the effect or property listing in the Properties panel, as in the illustration on page 115. The eyeball will disappear and so will the effect's change on your video image. To turn the effect back on, click the same spot. The eyeball icon will return and the effect will be again turned on.

To remove an effect from a clip, right-click on the effect's listing in the Properties panel and select Delete Selected Effect, or click to select the effect and click the trashcan icon at the bottom of the panel.

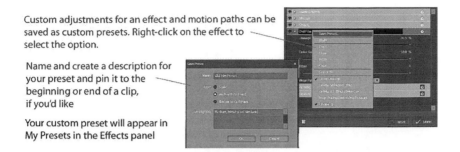

Custom adjustments for an effect and motion paths can be saved as custom presets. Right-click on the effect to select the option.

Name and create a description for your preset and pin it to the beginning or end of a clip, if you'd like

Your custom preset will appear in My Presets in the Effects panel

Saving a Custom Preset

Once you've adjusted or even keyframed an effect or property (To learn more about keyframing and creating motion paths, see **Chapter 13: Keyframing**), you can save it as a preset so that you can use it on another clip, even in another project. To do this, right-click on the effect's listing in the Properties panel and select Save Preset.

The option screen will then prompt you to name your preset. If your effect includes a keyframed motion, the screen will ask you if you'd like to set that motion to happen at the beginning or end of any clip you apply it to. Make your selections and then click okay to save the Preset.

The new Preset will be available under **My Presets**, on the drop-down menu in the Effects panel. (See **Chapter 8: The Effects Panel** for more information.) You can apply this preset to any clip, just as you can apply an effect or any of the default presets. Applying the preset to a clip automatically applies the motion path or effect, at the settings you initially created, including any keyframing you've added to it.

Paste Attributes

A quick and easy way to apply an adjusted effect, or even a keyframed motion, to several clips is to use **Paste Attributes**. Right-click on a clip on the timeline to which effects or keyframes have been added and select Copy. Then select another clip or group of clips, right-click and select Paste Attributes. All of the original clip's effects, adjustments and keyframed action will be applied to all of the selected clips!

Chapter 13
Keyframing
Creating special effects and motion paths

Keyframing is the system that Premiere Elements uses to set and control motion and effects that change settings over time. With keyframing, you can control the level of an effect or the scale and/or position of a clip at precise points throughout the duration of the clip. You can raise and lower the audio level at precise points; you can create motion paths for panning and zooming around a photo; you can even control, at precise points in any clip, the intensity or movement of a special effect. All of these are functions of keyframing.

The principle is a simple one: You indicate which points (keyframes) on your clip represent settings for a position, scale, effect or level of effect and the program automatically generates the frames between those points.

You can, for instance, using Scale and Position settings, set one keyframe point to display a close-up of one corner of a still photo in your video frame and then set the Scale and Position of the next keyframe point to display the entire photo. Premiere Elements will then automatically create the smooth motion path between those two position, seeming to zoom out from the corner to a view of the entire photo.

With Premiere Elements, you can add any number of keyframes to a clip, creating as much motion or variations in your effects settings as you'd like.

But the real power of this tool is in how easy it is to revise and adjust those positions and settings, giving you, the user, the ability to fine tune your path or effect until it is precisely the effect you want to achieve.

Although there are other workspaces in which you can create and edit keyframes (See **Adjusting Audio Levels on the Timeline**, in **Chapter 11: The Timeline/Sceneline Panel**), most of your keyframing work will likely be done on the Properties panel.

Open the Properties panel by clicking on the list icon at the top center of your timeline or sceneline or right-clicking on a clip on your timeline or sceneline and selecting Show Properties. (For more information about opening the Properties panel for a clip and adjusting effects, see **Chapter 12: The Properties Panel**.)

Keyframing Effects vs. Applying Settings to an Entire Clip

Until you begin a keyframing session (by clicking **Toggle Animation**, as described below), any positioning, scaling or settings you make for an effect or property in the Properties panel will apply to the *entire* clip. In other words, if you change the Scale to 50%, your entire clip will appear at 50% of its size.

However, once you click Toggle Animation and turn on keyframing, every movement generates a keyframe point at the position of the CTI (Current Time Indicator) on your timeline. It becomes a sort of waypoint for your effect or motion path. When you create another keyframe point later in the clip and apply other settings to it, the program creates a path of motion or transition between the two points.

Beginning a Keyframe Session

When you first open the Properties panel for a clip, the keyframing workspace is hidden. To reveal this workspace in the Properties panel timeline, click on the **Show Keyframes** button (the stopwatch icon with the arrow pointing left) in the upper right of the panel, as illustrated on the next page. You can widen the display of this timeline by dragging on the edge between the timeline area and the effects and properties listings.

This is your workspace for creating, adjusting and editing your keyframes. The time positions on this timeline represent positions, in time, on the clip itself. In fact, if you're editing in timeline mode, you'll notice that, as you move the CTI on the Properties panel timeline, the CTI on your project's main timeline moves in sync with it.

Accessing and understanding the Properties panel and the keyframing workspace

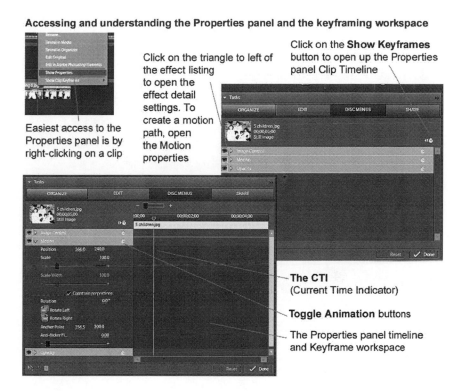

Easiest access to the Properties panel is by right-clicking on a clip

Click on the triangle to left of the effect listing to open the effect detail settings. To create a motion path, open the Motion properties

Click on the **Show Keyframes** button to open up the Properties panel Clip Timeline

The CTI
(Current Time Indicator)

Toggle Animation buttons

The Properties panel timeline and Keyframe workspace

To demonstrate how to use keyframes, we'll create a simple motion path – a pan and zoom from the middle of a photo.

With the Properties panel open and a still photo clip selected on timeline or sceneline, click on the triangle to the left of the Motion property listing to reveal the settings for Motion: Position, Scale and Rotation. Now turn on keyframing for the property by clicking on the Toggle Animation button for Motion (the stopwatch at the right end of the effect or property listing). When you click on the Toggle Animation button, a keyframe point, or set of keyframe points, is automatically created at the position of the CTI representing the current settings for that effect.

Now move the CTI to a new position, a few seconds to the right, on the clip's Properties panel timeline and, again, change the Position and Scale settings either by changing the setting numbers or by clicking on the clip in the Monitor panel and

A Simple Motion Path Created with Keyframes

CTI at beginning of clip

Clicking Toggle Animation creates
keyframe points for all settings
for the effect or property

When CTI is in new
position, any change to
any setting automatically
creates new keyframe

Line represents path
of motion in pan & zoom

Details of Properties panel Motion settings

Toggle Animation button

Position is horizontal and vertical measurements
(in pixels) to center of on-screen image

Scale is percentage size of clip has been
increased or decreased

Jump CTI to previous keyframe point on timeline

Create new keyframe point at CTI's current position

Jump to next keyframe point on timeline

As with most effects, Motion's Position and Scale
settings can be changed numerically, here, or
by clicking on the image in the Monitor and
dragging it to a new position or resizing it by
dragging on the corner points.

dragging the screen image to a new position or dragging on
its corner handles. As you change the settings at this new CTI
position, new keyframe points will automatically be generated on
the Properties panel timeline. (Note that you can also manually
create new keyframes by clicking on the diamond-shaped
keyframe creator buttons to the right of each effect's setting.)

You have just created a simple motion path! If you play back
the clip, you can see how the program creates the movement
between the keyframe points, using your keyframed positions to
define the path.

Easily Editable

The beauty of the keyframing tool is that any motion path or effects transition is infinitely adjustable. By dragging the keyframe points closer together or further apart on the Properties panel timeline, we can control the speed at which the motion occurs. We can add more keyframe points and/or delete the ones we don't want. And, if we really want to go deep, we

Using Keyframes to change effects settings over time

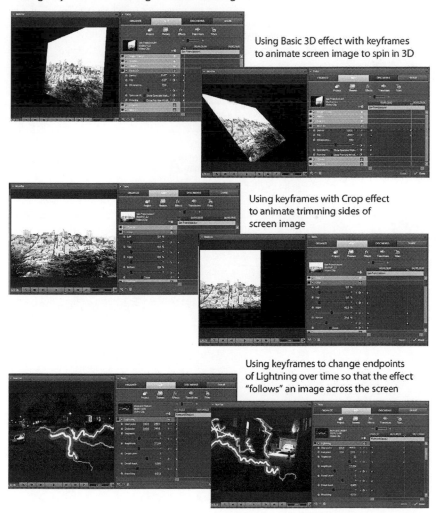

Using Basic 3D effect with keyframes to animate screen image to spin in 3D

Using keyframes with Crop effect to animate trimming sides of screen image

Using keyframes to change endpoints of Lightning over time so that the effect "follows" an image across the screen

can even use Bezier control handles to change the shape of the motion path or, by right-clicking on any point, vary the speed throughout the motion.

Many Applications

Keyframing is also used to control audio volume levels at precise points in your video project. (For more on controlling audio levels with keyframes, **Adjusting Audio Levels on the Timeline** in **Chapter 11: The Timeline/Sceneline Panel**).

With keyframing, you can also control effects, such as Crop, so that the area of your image that's cropped widens or narrows as the clip plays, as illustrated on the previous page. Or you can very precisely increase or decrease the intensity of an effect on a clip or animate a Picture-in-Picture effect (See **L-cuts, J-cuts and Multiple Tracks** in **Chapter 11: The Timeline/Sceneline Panel**). We can even use keyframes to create an animated 3D movement for our video image using the Camera View effect so that our video images seems to tumble head over heels in space.

Indeed, mastering the keyframing tool is the key to getting to the deeper aspects of Premiere Elements. It may not seem intuitive at first but, once you developed a feel for how it works, you'll soon find yourself able to see all kinds applications for it in creating and refining all manner of visual and audio effects.

For more information on some of the deeper aspects of keyframing and their applications, see my *Steve's Tips* articles "Advanced Keyframing: Editing on the Properties Panel Timeline" and "Advanced Keyframing 2: Keyframing Effects", available on the products page at Muvipix.com.

Chapter 14
Creating Disc Menus
For DVDs and BluRay discs

Although the DVD and BluRay menu authoring system in Premiere Elements isn't as advanced as is in many standalone disc menu authoring programs, such as Adobe's Encore, you can do a surprising amount just using Premiere Elements 7's library of disc menu templates and customization features.

Once you've applied and customized your disc menus, you can then create a DVD or BluRay disc using the options under the Share tab, as described in **Disc – Burn DVD and BluRay Discs** in **Chapter 15: Share.**

The Basics

Premiere Elements comes bundled with well over 100 standard templates, in categories from Entertainment to Travel to Sports to Kids to Birthdays and Weddings, from playful to serious to more artistic. Many of these templates come complete with audio and/or video loops that add life to your menus. Also, since version 4, many of these templates also include a "drop zone," a designated area on the menu where you can place a video clip or still. (More about that later.)

To apply a disc menu template to your project, click on the Disc Menus tab on the Tasks panel and select Templates. As with many workspaces in Premiere Elements 7, you can work from the library of materials included with the program or, by selecting the option from the panel's drop-down menu, you can go directly to any category of templates or even access additional products from Photoshop.com. (For more information on logging onto Photoshop.com, see **Photoshop.com** in **Chapter 2: Starting a Premiere Elements 7 Project.**)

Premiere Elements offers dozens of high-quality, easily customizable menus for your DVDs and BluRay discs in a wide variety of categories.

When you initially launch this workspace, the Monitor will be replaced by the Disc Layout monitor, and the Tasks panel will display the library of disc menu templates. You can filter this list by selecting a category of templates from the panel's category drop-down menu. Then you can browse the templates in the panel or go directly to a specific template by selecting it from the second drop-down menu (which displays Show All by default). Once you've selected a template by clicking on it, click the Apply button in the lower right of the panel.

If you've not yet added menu markers to your project's timeline or sceneline, you will be prompted to create menu markers. If you chose to create menu markers, you'll be prompted with some automatic options. If you choose not to include menu markers, your template will generate a menu with a main menu page only. If you choose not to include menu markers at the time and you later add a menu marker, a scene menu will be then generated for you. (For more information on creating menu markers for your project, see **Add Menu Markers** in **Chapter 11: The Timeline/Sceneline Panel**.)

Once you've applied a template, the Disc Layout panel will display your entire menu set as thumbnails in Disc Menus preview window at the bottom of the panel. The program will add as many extra pages as you need to accommodate all of your menu markers.

The Disc Layout panel's main window will display your main menu. If you click on any of the menu page thumbnails in the Disc Menus window, that menu will appear in the big Disc Layout window. The names you've given to your main and scene menu markers as well as the buttons you've created to represent these markers will appear on the menus. (For more information on menu markers, see **Add Menu Makers** in **Chapter 11: The Timeline/Sceneline Panel.**)

To see your menu system in action and test drive the links embedded in it, click the Preview button.

An important note about this Disc Layout Preview: It's not mean to be a true representation of your final menu template, and you'll probably be disappointed with the quality of the picture onscreen. Remember, though, that this is just a *preview*, created on the fly. It's not meant to represent the *quality* of the final menu image. Rather, the purpose of the preview is to allow you to see a representation of how your elements will come together and to allow you to test the navigation buttons.

Customizing Your Menu

Adobe has made it very easy to customize your menus right in this Disc Menus workspace. In fact, once you've applied a

The Disc Menu Customization Workspace

Click to replace background of menu with your own still or video loop

Set at which point in clip to begin video loop

Click to replace or add your own audio loop

Set duration for video/audio loop (max of 30 seconds)

Background has been selected

Menu previews

Click to play preview of menu

Click for no menus

Check to apply custom background and audio to all menus

template, as described above, in the Disc Menus workspace, the panel will change from a view of the templates library to a menu customization workspace. (If, as you're working, this workspace is replaced with another workspace, you can recall it by clicking on background of the menu displayed in the Disc Layout monitor.)

The Menu Background panel in this customization workspace allows you to swap out the current template's background image with a photo or even a loop of a video clip of your choosing. To do so, simply click the Browse button and browse to a video clip or photo on your computer. If you're using a video clip, you can use the In Point timecode (either by dragging your mouse across the numbers or by playing to a particular point) to set your video loop to begin at a specific point in the clip.

(Note that some menu templates include foreground graphics that will remain, even if you swap out the background and may partially cover your new background. If you'd prefer not to include these graphics in your menus, you may want to start with one of the Generic templates, such as the one in the General set.)

Likewise, you can add or swap out audio loops that play as your menus are displayed. And, likewise, you can direct that the loop to begin playing at any point in the song.

Above, a new background clip has replaced the template background. When a text block is selected, the customization menu changes to a font, style and text color selection option screen.

A before-and-after look at a customized Premiere Elements menu

You can go back to the default background, music or sound by clicking on the appropriate Reset button.

Below these customization options, you'll find a control for setting the duration of your audio and video loops. The maximum duration for these loops is 30 seconds, which is standard even for professionally produced discs. After all, you want your audience to watch your movie, not waste several minutes watching your menu, right?

Customizing the Text

You can also customize any of the text used in your disc menus.

Click to select any text on your menus in the Disc Layout main window and the text customization workspace will display in the Tasks panel. Using this menu, you can change the font, font size and even color of the text. The Apply to All Text Items button will apply the font and text style across all of the text that appears on this menu page.

Once you've customized the look of your text, you can also customize its position on the menu. Just click on the text block on the Disc Layout monitor and drag it to where you'd like it to appear. On your scene menus, you can move the scene buttons themselves. You can also drag any of these button by their corner handles to resize them.

Drop Zones

An exciting feature included with some disc menu templates is a "drop zone." These are designated areas of a menu template into which you can place your own pictures or video. You'll find examples of this in the Movie Genre/Fairytale template and the Wedding/Outdoor Wedding template.

Once you've applied one of these templates, you can add a clip to the drop zone (the area labeled "Add Your Media Here") by clicking on the menu's background and then browsing to replace the background with an image or video on your computer. Once you've replaced it, hold the Shift key and drag the corner handles of this new background to resize and position it as you'd like. (Holding the Shift key constrains the proportions so that the clip resizes proportionately.)

A menu template that includes a "drop zone" for containing a still or video clip

The "Add Your Media Here" graphic is usually a guide for placement, based on the other graphics in the template. In most cases, you can size and place the your new background clip wherever you'd like. An exception would be the General/Fun template, in which you'll need to size and position your clip pretty precisely in order for it to display in the template's provided picture box.

Chapter 15
Share
Output options in Premiere Elements 7

Once you've finished your video masterpiece and, if you're planning to output it to disc, you have applied and customized your disc's menus, as described in **Chapter 14: Creating Disc Menus,** you're ready to output your video so that you can share it with the world. There are a number of ways to output from Premiere Elements 7, and a surprisingly large number of formats you can output to.

A click on the green Share tab reveals a list of five destinations for your video, each of which offers recommended formats and settings for your output as well as more advanced settings for more advanced users. (If all five options don't show in this Share panel, you'll need to resize the panel by dragging on the boundaries between it and the adjoining panels.)

Disc – Burn DVD and BluRay Discs

Probably the most common way to output a movie from your Premiere Elements project is to burn a DVD or high-definition BluRay disc. To access these output options, click to select the Disc option.

Premiere Elements will burn to both single-layer and dual-layer discs and both standard DVD and BluRay formats. (The program automatically scans your system to see which disc burner hardware you have and if you have a disc in the drive.) Click to select the disc type you want to create from the listing at the top of the panel. If you are burning a DVD, the Burn To drop-down menu will allow you to select the option to burn directly to a disk or to burn your DVD files to a folder on your hard drive for either a single-layer or dual-layer disk.

The Share panel in Premiere Elements 7 divides its output options among five destinations.

Type the name for your project in the space provided. (This is more important if you plan to burn your disc files to a folder on your hard drive, as described below.)

As a rule of thumb, you can fit about 70 minutes of video onto a standard (4.7 gigabyte) DVD at full video quality and about double that onto a dual layer disc. A BluRay disc (which can store 25 gigabytes of data) can hold about two hours of hi-definition video, while a dual-layer BluRay disc can hold about twice that. If you put more than these recommended capacities on a disc, Premiere Elements will automatically reduce the quality of the video as needed if you have the Fit Contents option checked. (This reduced quality may not be noticeable unless you try to squeeze considerably more content onto the disc than the optimal capacity.)

In a perfect world, outputting a disk from Premiere Elements would be as simple as selecting the options at this screen and hitting the Burn button. Unfortunately, your computer's operating system is something of a living, continually evolving environment, with programs constantly at war for control over your hardware. And failures to burn directly to a disc with

Although this is becoming less of an issue as creating home-burned DVDs and BluRay discs has become more popular, it's important to realize that not all DVD and BluRay players can play home-burned discs. This is because the process used to create commercial discs (pressing) is very different than the process you use to create discs on your computer (a chemical process). Manufacturers have recognized the growing popularity of creating home-burned DVDs and BluRay discs and have been making their players more and more compatible to them. But be prepared for the occasional friend or client who simply can't play a disc you created.

this program are somewhat common – which can be quite frustrating if you've waited hours for the program to encode your disk files, only to have it suddenly throw up an error code.

If this is a problem for you (and you'll know because the operation will fail in its very last stages) the simplest solution is to go to the Burn To drop-down menu and select the option to burn your files to folder on your hard drive rather directly to a disc, then click the Burn button in the bottom right of the panel. Once these DVD or BluRay files are created, you can then easily use your computer's disc burning software (Nero, RecordNow, etc.) to burn the folders of files the program creates to a DVD or BluRay disk. This process is detailed in **The "Burn Disc" Workaround** in the **Appendix**.

Most output options include a recommended preset and several alternative presets

The Share Work Area Bar Only options allows you to output only a designated portion of your video project

Many output options also include Advanced settings

In half-tone text, the program will also provide you information on the technical specs of our output file

Along with the options to burn a DVD or BluRay disc, Premiere Elements can be set to burn to a folder on your hard drive.

Although this may seem like an unnecessary workaround at first, there are a number advantages to using this two-step method for creating discs and very few liabilities. (It certainly doesn't take any more time, and it only adds a few clicks to the process.) If nothing else, it makes outputting several copies of your disc easy, since creating each will be a simple matter of burning these same files (a process which takes just a few minutes) to another disc.

And, if for no other reason than because direct burns to disc can so commonly fail, we at Muvipix recommend doing it as a two-stop process. It really is worth the minimal extra effort to ensure the job gets done.

You can also increase the odds your disc burn will go smoothly and that your disc will be compatible with every possible DVD or BluRay player by using high-quality media. Verbatim and Taiyo Yuden are two very reliable disc brands. Store brands, and even other popular name brands, can be a bit iffier. In our not-so-humble opinion, the little extra expense you'll incur by using one of these two brands will be more than offset by the knowledge that you'll get the best possible results and compatibility from them.

Also, *NEVER* stick a label onto your DVD or BluRay disc! Labels can throw the spin and balance off when the disks are loaded into a player and the glue and label can damage the media itself. If you'd like to customize your disks, we recommend that you buy printable disks and use a good inkjet printer with disk printing capabilities. Epson and HP make very nice printers with this feature for under $100.

Online – Upload to YouTube or Other Websites

The Online output option is designed to transcode your video to another file format and upload it to a web site (including YouTube and Photoshop.com, if you have an account) in one easy step.

Once you've selected the site you'd like to upload to from the listing at the top of the panel, fill in the blanks, including your user name, password and server name, as applicable.

The Presets drop-down menu, by default, will display the optimal file format for uploading. You can also drop-down this menu and select another option.

Online options let you load your video directly to a web site, including video sharing sites like YouTube and Photoshop.com

If your option isn't listed, click the Back button in the lower right corner of the panel and create your video using the Personal Computer option, as described below.

Checking the Share Work Area Bar Only option will export only the portion of your video designated by Work Area Bar. (For more information, see **The Work Area Bar** in **Chapter 11: The Timeline/Sceneline Pane**l.)

Once you've set all of your options, click the Next button in the lower right of the panel and you'll be directed to a login and upload screen for the site you've selected.

As with many automatic functions, this one may not always work as smoothly as it should. (This is mostly because sites, like YouTube, are constantly changing the way they handle uploaded files.) And, if you have trouble getting your video directly to a site, you can click the Back button in the lower right corner of the panel and select the Personal Computer output option instead. You can then save your video to your computer and upload it using the site's upload screen or using FTP utility software such as the excellent shareware WS_FTP or the easy-to-use freeware Easy FTP.

Personal Computer – Export Files for Viewing on Computers
The subtitle to this output option is a little misleading. You not only can use this output option to output video for viewing

The most versatile output destination is Personal Computer, which allows you to save your video as a Flash, MPEG, DV-AVI, Windows Media or Quicktime (MOV) file

on a computer, but you can use it to save to any of the five main video output formats. In other words, you can not only output videos from this option for PC-based viewing, but you can also create videos that you can then post to web sites, e-mail, etc. Also, this is where you find the option to output the all-important DV-AVI (full quality video) file, as explained in **Exporting Video to be Used in Another Editing Project**, below.

Next to each file format listing in this Share output category is a descriptor explaining the best use for that particular file format. We've also included a discussion of the each file format in detail in **Video Output Formats**, later in this chapter.

A number of these file formats are used for displaying your video on the Web (Flash, or **FLV** files; Windows Media, or **WMV** files; and, Quicktime, or **MOV** files.) Once you've output any of these file types to your computer's hard drive, you can then use FTP software (such as the excellent WS_FTP) or your Web site's upload software to post the video to a site. This is an excellent workaround if, for some reason, the Online output option doesn't work, as discussed above. See our **Appendix** for more information on these excellent FTP utilities.

Once you select a file format, the Presets drop-down list will display the recommended file compression setting for that output type. If you prefer another setting, you can drop down that list and select a different compression setting or click on the Advanced button to access deeper settings.

Once you've selected your output option, click the Browse button to select a location on your computer for your file to be saved.

Checking the Share Work Area Bar Only option will export only the portion of your video designated by Work Area Bar.

(For more information, see **The Work Area Bar** in **Chapter 11: The Timeline/Sceneline Panel**.)

When you've selected all of your options, click the Save button in the lower right corner of the panel.

Mobile Phones and Players – Export Files for Viewing on Mobile Phones and Other Devices

Selecting this output option directs you to a screen on which are listed all of the major mobile devices for viewing video, from iPods and Zunes to Pocket PCs, iPods and Smartphones. (You may need to scroll the list to see the entire listing.) Whichever you choose, the program will recommend the optimal preset for

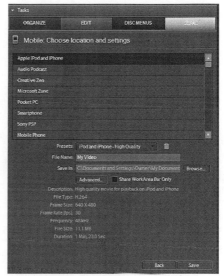

Output options to mobile devices include a variety of presets for many popular devices, including H.264/MPEG4s for both video and audio and WMVs for the Microsoft Zune.

that device. You can, however, select other options from the Preset drop-down menu or click the Advanced button for deeper settings. A discussion of each file option is in **Video Output Options,** below.

Type your file name in the space provided and click the Browse button to select the location on your computer that you'd like to save your file. You can also save directly to your device.

Checking the Share Work Area Bar Only option will export only the portion of your video designated by Work Area Bar. (For more information, see **The Work Area Bar** in **Chapter 11: The Timeline/Sceneline Panel**.)

When you've selected all of your options, click the Save button in the lower right corner of the panel.

Tape – Sending your video back to your camcorder

Now that DVDs and BluRay discs have become so popular, it's much less common to send completed projects back to tape. However, there's still no better way to archive your finished project in a high-quality, re-editable format than to send it back to the same device that created it in the first place. Remember, miniDV and HDV camcorders and video editing programs speak the same language, so saving your finished project back to tape is a cheap and convenient way to store 13 gigabytes of high-quality, re-editable video data.

Exporting Video to be Used in Another Editing Project

If you'd like to export your video project – or even a portion of your project – so that you can import it in another Premiere Elements project, your best Share format is the DV-AVI, available as a Personal Computer Share option. The ideal source file for Premiere Elements and the universal language for PC-based video editors, DV-AVIs maintain virtually all of the quality of your original source footage.

This is also the file format you use to create file segments when you're working on a large project in small parts – the most efficient way to work on a longer movie. Just break your movie project into ten or 15 minute "chapters" which, when completed, you output as DV-AVIs and then gather into one big, final mix project. Doing this can minimize system lugging and maximize program responsiveness as well as reduce the likelihood that you'll run into problems when you try to export your video as a DVD or BluRay disc.

With the DV-AVI output option selected, type your file name in the space provided and click the Browse button to select the location on your computer that you'd like to save your file.

You can also quickly output a DV-AVI of your Premiere Elements project by clicking to select the Timeline/Sceneline Panel then, from the File drop-down menu at the top of the program, selecting Export, Movie and browsing to a location to save your video file. To minimize compression artifacts, before you save the file, click the Settings button and, at the Video tab, uncheck the Recompress option.

Checking the Share Work Area Bar Only option will export only the portion of your video designated by Work Area Bar. (For more information, see **The Work Area Bar** in **Chapter 11: The Timeline/Sceneline Panel**.)

When you've selected all of your options, click the Save button in the lower right corner of the panel.

Video Output Formats

The six main video output formats available under the Share tab are **DV-AVI**s, **MPEG**s, **WMV**s (Windows Media Video), **FLV**s (Flash video), **MOV**s (Quicktime) and **MP4**s, and you'll find at least one of these options offered as the best solution at each of the output destinations.

Here's what each file format is and what its main benefits and liabilities are:

DV-AVIs are the "purest" and highest quality video output format, though the files are considerably larger than the other options. (It's the file format that outputs from a miniDV camcorder and/or is created as part of the workflow within the program.) This format is your best choice for creating an editable video output; for example if you were outputting your project, or a segment of your project, for use as part of another video editing project. DV-AVIs are the universal language of PC-based video editors, the perfect balance of compression and file size for working with on a computer.

MPEGs are a high quality video delivery format. This means that they play at nearly the quality of your original footage. (A form of MPEG, called a VOB file, is the format used to store the video on a DVD.) However, because it is a much smaller video file, it is also highly compressed and can be challenging to re-edit later. As a general rule, you should think of MPEGs as a delivery format rather than an editing or re-editing format.

WMVs, MOVs and **FLVs** are generally considered to be web formats, because they are highly compressed and often have reduced frame rates and frame sizes (most often 320x240 pixels, or about one-fourth the size of your original video) in order to produce the smallest, most efficient file sizes.

Currently, WMVs (Windows Media Video) are considered the Internet standard for web video because Microsoft's ubiquitous presence means that virtually every computer in the world has the necessary software to play them.

MOVs (Apple's Quicktime format) are also fairly ubiquitous (though PC users must load the Quicktime player manually the first time they play one), and Apple's efforts to continually improve the format means that often it can produce a higher quality video than WMVs.

FLVs (Flash video files) are gaining tremendous popularity on the internet, thanks to video sharing sites, like YouTube, which appreciate the fact that FLVs produce excellent video quality while using minimal internet bandwith.

If you select Mobile Phones and Players as your Share option, you'll have access to yet another file format output – the default output option for iPods and iPhones, Audio Podcasts and Mobile Phone. Using the **H.264** compression codec, this file format is also known as simply the **MP4**. (The Mobile Phone destination will also output an MP4, however, it uses the slightly less sophisticated H.263 codec.)

H.264 and H.263 are advanced compression systems that can produce very high quality video and audio but can do so with remarkably small files. The H.263 option for Mobile Phone produces a file that, by default, is a mere 176x144 pixels – fine for a mobile phones but a rather small frame for, say, playback on a computer. The H.264 option for iPod and iPhone, however, produces video at a full 640x480 pixels and 30 fps, the same size and frame rate as an AVI, but at a reduced size. True, with that kind of compression, the files do suffer a slight loss of picture quality. But, regardless, this is an ideal format for mobile devices which support it.

Appendix

Recommended computer specs

The rule of thumb for figuring the minimal computer specs to run a program is to take the minimums recommended by the manufacturer and double them. That's certainly true in the case of Premiere Elements, for which Adobe vastly understates the power needed to run this program effectively.

Virtually any computer made in the last couple of years will run Premiere Elements just fine – although laptops, which tend to be built for portability rather than power, often cost about 50% more for the same power as a desktop equivalent. They also tend to have limited hard drive space and smaller monitors than desktops. So, if you do decide to edit on a laptop, be ready and willing to put down the extra cash for the necessary power and hardware.

Here are our recommended minimums specs for running this program with standard DV.

- Pentium 4 or 2.6 ghz or Athlon64 3200
- 2 gigabytes of RAM (3-4 gigabytes for Vista)
- 128 mb video card, ideally ATI or nVidia technology
- 100 gigabyte of free hard drive (This allows plenty of room for captured footage and scratch disk space)
- An ASIO (Audio Stream Input/Output) supported sound card
- DVD burner
- 19" monitor set to at least a 1280x960 display (dual-monitors are even better)
- IEEE-1394/FireWire/iLink connection

High-definition video takes considerably more power to edit, since it uses a more highly-compressed file to store four times as much video data in the same amount of space as standard DV. For that reason, we recommend these minimums for hi-def editing.

- Intel dual-core at 2.0 ghz or Athlon64 Dual Core 4200
- 4 gigabytes of RAM
- 128 mb video card, ideally ATI or nVidia technology
- DVD or, better, BluRay DVD burner
- 19" monitor set to at least a 1280x960 display
  (a 22" widescreen or dual 19" monitors is even better)
- IEEE-1394/FireWire/iLink connection

The addition of a second hard drive (either internal or external), one dedicated to your video projects and source files, can give your workflow a tremendous boost. Not only does it often make the process go more smoothly, since it keeps the video data flow and scratch disk files separate from your operating system's paging files, but it also reduces fragmentation of your video files.

If you install an internal second hard drive for video editing, make sure to set it up in your BIOS (the set-up that displays before the operating system launches, when you first start your computer) as well as in your operating system.

Vista or XP?

XP is definitely a high point in Microsoft's operating system's evolution. So, if you've got it on your system and it's running well, there's no reason to upgrade.

Vista, on the other hand, has gotten a largely undeserved bad rap since its release last year, despite it also being a very solid operating system. Keep it updated and keep your drivers and firmware as up to date as possible (as we recommend below) and your performance on Vista should continue to improve as hardware manufacturers (and third party providers, like Apple) continue to provide improved support for it.

Both Vista and XP can benefit from a bit of tweaking though. And the simple tweaks below will help ensure you're getting the most from system's resources.

And, whether you use an internal or external drive, make sure that the drive is formatted NTFS rather than FAT32 (which all drives are factory formatted as by default) in order to avoid FAT32's file size limitations. Converting a drive from FAT32 to NTFS is easy and you won't lose any data already on the drive in the process. The instructions for doing so are available all over the Web, including on the Microsoft site.

Optimizing XP for video editing

1. Right-click My Computer and select Properties to bring up your System Properties panel. Under the Advanced tab, click the Settings button at Performance. Under the Visual Effects tab, uncheck all but (to keep the XP look) "Use visual styles on windows and buttons." Under the Advanced tab, make sure Processor Scheduling and Memory Usage are set to programs.

2. Click on Virtual Memory. For the most part, XP does a very good job of allocating Virtual Memory, so checking System Managed will work fine. Some people, however, recommend setting VM manually. If you'd prefer, set both the Minimum and Maximum to 1½ times your RAM load. Then click Set.

3. Open My Computer and right-click on your hard drive(s) and choose Properties. At the Hard Drive Properties window, uncheck both Compress Drive to Save Space and Allow Indexing Service. (The Indexing Service, which logs every new file added to your drive, frequently interrupts intensive processes such as captures.)

You'll need to reboot for these settings to take effect.

Optimizing Vista for best performance

1. From Start, go to your Control Panel, then select Performance Information and Tools. In the dialog box that opens, select Indexing Options in the left pane. Then, click the Modify button in the Indexing Options dialog box and click the Show All Locations button at the bottom of the Indexed Locations dialog box. For best performance, turn off Indexing on all of your drives.

2. Click Start, right-click on Computer, and click Properties. Click Advanced System Settings. Click on the Advanced tab. Under Performance, click Settings. Uncheck these options:

- Fade or slide menus into view
- Fade or slide tooltips into view
- Fade out menu items after clicking
- Show shadows under menus
- Slide open combo boxes
- Slide taskbar buttons
- Use a background image for each folder type

Close the Performance Options & System Properties dialogs.

3. Windows Vista Sidebar provides instant access to gadgets. However, the Sidebar is one of Vista's top resource suckers. Turn it off and your computer will sigh in relief.

4. Turn off the Aero interface! Right-click on your desktop, select Properties and then Appearance. Select the basic Vista look. It may not be quite as cool as Aero's semi-transparent windows, but it's well worth the trade-off in performance. And, in two days, you probably won't miss it anyway.

Maintain your computer

Your computer doesn't just seem to run slower as it ages, it often *does* run slower. This is due to the accumulation of data 'sludge' on your hard drive – temp files and bits of pieces of programs you've installed and/or removed from your system. Additionally, any time spent on the Internet loads your hard drive with cache files, cookies and, often, spyware.

The regimen below will help keep your computer running like new. Think of it as cleaning the dust bunnies out of your system.

And, at the very least, keep Windows updated and check the Apple site regularly to ensure you have the latest version of Quicktime! Quicktime plays an important role in Premiere Elements' function, and a surprising number of problems (such as video not displaying in the monitor while capturing) can be cured simply by loading the newest version.

Do this weekly:

1. Go to Microsoft Update and make sure Windows is updated. In fact, don't just check for priority updates, click on the **Custom** button and look for other updates (like RealTek drivers) that may not update automatically. You may not need everything offered, but it certainly doesn't hurt to have them.

2. Make sure your virus software is updated. (If your virus software isn't set to run in the middle of the night, waking your computer from sleep, for a virus scan, you also may want to do a regular virus scan.) And, every once in a while, go to the web site for your virus software and make sure you have the latest *VERSION* of the anti-virus software. You may have the latest virus definitions added automatically – but, if you're still using last year's version of the software, you could still be vulnerable.

3. With XP, use the excellent free downloads Spybot Search & Destroy and Spyware Blaster to clear off and block spyware. (Update them before you use them and, regularly, check their web sites to make sure you're using the latest versions before you run them.) You can pick both up from the links on this page: http://savemybutt.com/downloads.html

   Vista includes a program called Defender that does an excellent job of blocking spyware on its own. In most cases, then, you won't need to do any extra spyware maintenance on a Vista machine.

4. Run the free, excellent, easy-to-use tool Advanced Windows Care to tune up your registry and clear off temp and other files that are just taking up space. This program also is available at http://savemybutt.com/downloads.html

5. Run the Defragmenter on all of your hard drives. And don't forget to back up your files (at least the My Documents folder) regularly! Remember, the one piece of hardware on your computer that absolutely *WILL* eventually fail is your hard drive. If you're lucky, you'll have replaced your computer before then. But if not – please remember to back up your files regularly.

Do this monthly:

1. Check your graphic's card's manufacturer's site, your sound card's manufacturer's site and, if applicable, the RealTek site to make sure your drivers and firmware are up to date. Also, double-check the Apple site to ensure you have the latest version of Quicktime.

2. Go to your web browser and clear the cache. In IE7, you'll find the option for doing this right under the Tools drop-down. Older versions and other browsers (including Firefox) keep them under Tools and in Internet Options. You can leave the cookies – but do delete the Temporary Internet Files. Accumulate enough of them and they will slow your entire computer system.

Valuable Free or Low Cost Tools and Utilities
Video Conversion Tools

All video may look the same and sound the same, but it actually comes in many flavors, formats and compression systems (codecs). Premiere Elements is built around a DV-AVI workflow. (DV-AVIs are AVI files that use the DV codec.) This means that DV-AVIs flow easily through it and place the least strain on the program and, ultimately, your system. Not all AVIs use the DV codec, and many (such as video from still cameras) can cause real problems for Premiere Elements.

A good rule of thumb is that, whenever possible, you should use DV-AVIs as your video source.

A number of free or low-cost programs will convert your files.

MPEG Streamclip (free at http://www.squared5.com.) - A great tool for easily converting MPEGs and VOB files (DVD video files). To use it, open the file with MPEG Streamclip and then open the AVI/DivX Exporter window from File/Export to AVI.

For Compression select the Apple DV/DVPRO_NTSC (or DV PAL, if appropriate) codec.

For Field Order select Lower Field First.

Change the default sound settings from MPEG Layer 3 to Uncompressed.

If you have widescreen footage click on the Options at the top right. Leave the Scan Mode as is but change the Aspect Ratio from 4:3 to 16:9.

If you would like to save these settings, click on the Presets button at the bottom left then click on the New button to name and save your settings. The next time you run MPEG Streamclip, you can go directly to the Presets button and Load your saved settings. Click on "Make AVI" and choose a folder and filename for your DV-AVI file.

Windows MovieMaker - It's right on your computer, and it handles a wide range of files. It's particularly good for converting still camera video to a format Premiere Elements can work with.

To convert a video into a DV-AVI with MovieMaker, simply import it into MovieMaker and drag it to the MovieMaker timeline. Then:

From the Main Menu select File/Save Movie File

A dialog will open - Select 'My Computer' and press the Next button.

On the next screen you can name the new file and select/ browse to a folder to put the file in (remember where you put it because you will need to browse to the file in Premiere Elements to import to you project). When you have named the file and selected the location press the Next button.

On the next screen, click the link that says Show More Choices. There will be three radio buttons to choose from. Select No. 3, Other Settings and, from the drop-down menu, select DV-AVI.

Quicktime Pro ($29 from Apple) - A great tool to own if you use a lot of MOVs (Quicktime) as source files. It not only converts MOVs to DV-AVIs but also includes some basic video editing functions.

VirtualDub (free from www.virtualdub.org) – This terrific tool should be on everyone's computer. Less a conversion tool than a video processor, it will make many AVIs (including

Type 1 DV-AVIs) compatible with Premiere Elements as well as converting many other file types.

Converting is as easy as opening the file in VirtualDub and doing a Save As to create the new, freshly-processed file.

Super (free from http://www.erightsoft.com/SUPER.html) - A great little all-purpose tool that converts nearly any major video format into virtually any other – and that includes MOV files and Divx AVIs. It's also very easy to use.

Capture Utilities

In the event Premiere Elements won't capture your video no matter what you do, these free or low-cost tools will capture compatible video files.

WinDV (free from http://windv.mourek.cz/) – A great capture utility with a simple interface.

HDVSplit (free from http://strony.aster.pl/paviko/hdvsplit) – A great capture utility for HDV video.

Scenalyzer ($30 from www.scenalyzer.com) – A low-cost capture utility with some great extra features.

Windows MovieMaker – Video captured from a miniDV camcorder into MovieMaker is perfectly compatible with Premiere Elements.

Nero – Sometimes Nero's presence on your computer is the *reason* you can't capture from Premiere Elements. However, if you've got it on your computer, you can use it to do your capture also.

If all else fails, you can use the software that came with your camcorder to capture your video. However, if this software will not capture your video as a DV-AVI (or MPEG2 for high-definition video) or convert to it, we recommend you convert your captured video using the software above before you bring it into a Premiere Elements project for best program performance.

Audio Utilities

Audacity is, hands down, the best free audio editing software you'll find anywhere. Easy to use, loaded with preset audio filters and yet extremely versatile, Audacity can convert audio formats as well as adjust audio levels and "sweeten" your audio's sound. You can also record into it from a microphone or external audio device and edit audio with it. A real must-have freebie that you'll find yourself going to regularly!

FTP Software

FTP software uploads files from your computer to a web site and downloads files from a site to your computer. There are many great applications out there. Here are a couple personal favorites.

WS_FTP (Free to try, then $39.95 from http://www.ipswitch.com/WS_FTP) – This used to be everyone's favorite FTP software. There used to be a free "LE" version, and it may still be available out on the web if you look for it.

Easy FTP (free from http://www.download.com and other sources) – Completely free and nearly as intuitive as WS_FTP.

The "Burn Disc" Workaround

In a perfect world, you could put together a project out of any media, click the Share tab and burn it to a disk. Unfortunately, for a variety of reasons – some related to Premiere Elements, most related to operating system drivers or program conflicts, this sometimes doesn't go as smoothly as it should.

The simplest solution is to break the process down into its elements and then troubleshoot each element individually.

There are three main reasons for a problem burning a DVD or BluRay disc: challenging source video (including photos that are larger than the recommended 1000x750 pixels in size); interfacing issues with your disc burner (often the result of a program like Nero not sharing the burner with other programs); and lack of computer resources (namely lack of available scratch disk space on your hard drive). This workaround eliminates most Burn Disc problems. And those it doesn't eliminate, it at least helps you isolate where the problem is occurring.

1. **Create a "pure" AVI project.** Click on the timeline panel and then go to File/Export/Movie to create an AVI of your entire project. If this works, do a Save As to save

a copy of your project, delete all of the video except this newly created AVI, then place the AVI on the timeline in place of the deleted video (the DVD markers should still line up).

If you are unable to create an AVI, it could be that your photos are too large or you lack the resources to render the files,as discussed below.

2. **Burn to a folder** rather than directly to a disc. Select this option from Share/Output/Disc. This eliminates the possibility that other disk burning software is interfering with communication with your computer's burner. Once the disk files are created, you can use your computer's burner software to burn the VIDEO_TS folder and its contents to a disk.

If this doesn't work, it could be that your computer lacks the necessary resources, as discussed below.

3. Clear space on and defragment your hard drive. A one-hour video can require up to 50 gigabytes of free, defragmented space on your hard drive to render and process (depending on your source files). Even a "pure" AVI project can require 20-30 gigabytes of space.

Clear off your computer and regularly defragment it, per **Maintain Your Computer**, above, and you'll reduce the likelihood of this being an issue – assuming you've got an adequately powered computer and an adequately large hard drive in the first place.

Keyboard Shortcuts

These key strokes and key combinations are great, quick ways to launch features or use the program's tools without having to poke around the interface.

In virtually every workspace the arrow keys (Down, Up, Left, Right) will move the selected object that direction. Shift+Arrow will move it several steps in one nudge.

Program Controls

Ctrl O	Open project	Ctrl X	Cut
Ctrl W	Close project	Ctrl C	Copy
Ctrl S	Save project	Ctrl V	Paste
Ctrl Shift S	Save project as...	Tab	Close floating windows
Ctrl Alt S	Save a copy	Ctrl Q	Quit program
Ctrl Z	Undo	F1	Help
Ctrl Shift Z	Redo		

Import/Export

F5	Capture		
Ctrl I	Add Media	Ctrl Alt Shift M	Export Audio
Ctrl M	Export Movie	Ctrl Shift H	Get properties for selection
Ctrl Shift M	Export Frame		

Media and Trimming

I	Set in point	G	Clear all in/out points
O	Set out point	D	Clear selected in point
Q	Go to in point	F	Clear selected out point
Page Down	Go to next edit point	Ctrl E	Edit original
W	Go to out point	Ctrl H	Rename
Page Up	Go to previous edit point		

Play/Scrub Controls

Space bar	Play/stop	Home	Go to beginning clip/ timeline
J	Shuttle left		
L	Shuttle right	End	Go to end clip/timeline
Shift J	Slow shuttle left	Q	Go to in point
Shift L	Slow shuttle right	W	Go to out point
K	Shuttle stop	Page Down	Go to next edit point
Arrow Left	One frame back	Page Up	Go to previous edit point
Arrow Right	One frame forward	Ctrl Alt Space	Play in point to out point with preroll/postroll
Shift Left	Step back five frames		
Shift Right	Step forward five frames		

Appendix

Timeline Controls

Enter	Render work area
Ctrl K	Razor cut at CTI
+	Zoom in
-	Zoom out
\	Zoom to work area
Ctrl A	Select all
Ctrl Shift A	Deselect all
, (comma)	Insert
. (period)	Overlay
Ctrl Shift V	Insert Clip
Alt [video clip]	Unlink audio/video
Ctrl G	Group
Ctrl Shift G	Ungroup
X	Time stretch
Del	Clear clip (non-ripple)
Backspace	Ripple delete (fill gap)
S	Toggle snap
C	Razor tool
V	Selection tool

Alt [	Set Work Area Bar In Point
Alt]	Set Work Area Bar Out Point
Ctrl Alt C	Copy attributes
Ctrl Alt V	Paste Attributes
Ctrl Shift /	Duplicate
Shift * (Num pad)	Set next unnumbered marker
* (Num pad)	Set unnumbered marker
Ctrl Shift Right	Go to next clip marker
Ctrl Shift Left	Go to previous clip marker
Ctrl Shift 0	Clear current marker
Alt Shift 0	Clear all clip markers
Ctrl Right	Go to next timeline marker
Ctrl Left	Go to previous timeline marker
Ctrl 0	Clear current timeline marker
Alt 0	Clear all timeline markers

Title Window Controls

Ctrl Shift L	Title type align left
Ctrl Shift R	Title type align right
Ctrl Shift C	Title type align center
Ctrl Shift T	Set title type tab
Ctrl Shift D	Position object bottom safe margin
Ctrl Shift F	Position object left safe margin
Ctrl Shift O	Position object top safe margin
Ctrl Alt Shift C	Insert copyright symbol
Ctrl Alt Shift R	Insert registered symbol
Ctrl J	Open title templates
Ctrl Alt]	Select object above
Ctrl Alt [	Select object below
Ctrl Shift]	Bring object to front

Ctrl [	Bring object forward
Ctrl Shift [	Send object to back
Ctrl [	Send object backward
Alt Shift Left	Decrease kerning five units
Alt Shift Right	Increase kerning five units
Alt Left	Decrease kerning one unit
Alt Right	Increase kerning one unit
Alt Shift Up	Decrease leading five unit
Alt Shift Down	Increase leading five units
Alt Up	Decrease leading one unit
Alt Down	Increase leading one unit
Ctrl Up	Decrease text size five points
Ctrl Down	Increase text size five points
Shift Up	Decrease text size one point
Shift Down	Increase text site one point

Media Window

Ctrl Delete	Delete selection with options	End	Move selection to last clip
Shift Down	Extend selection down	Page Down	Move selection page down
Shift Left	Extend selection left	Page Up	Move selection page up
Shift Up	Extend selection up	Right	Move selection right
Down	Move selection to next clip	Shift]	Thumbnail size next
Up	Move selection to previous clip	Shift [	Thumbnail size previous
Home	Move selection to first clip	Shift \	Toggle view

Capture Monitor Panel

F	Fast forward	Left	Step back
G	Get frame	Right	Step forward
R	Rewind	S	Stop

Properties Panel

Backspace	Delete selected effect

Narration Panel

Delete	Delete present narration clip	Space	Play present narration clip
Right	Go to next narration clip	G	Start/Stop recording
Left	Go to previous narration clip		

Note that Premiere Elements also allows you to modify any of these keyboard shortcuts and to create your own shortcuts for dozens of other tasks. You'll find the option to do so under the Edit drop-down menu.

Index

Index

Index

2963919

Made in the USA